WOODTURNING
Christmas Ornaments
WITH
Dale L. Nish

T0323156

WOODTURNING
Christmas Ornaments
<small>WITH</small>
Dale L. Nish

Dale L. Nish with Susan L. Hendrix

FOX CHAPEL
PUBLISHING

© 2012 by Dale L. Nish and Fox Chapel Publishing Company, Inc., 903 Square Street, Mount Joy, PA 17552.

Woodturning Christmas Ornaments with Dale L. Nish is an original work, first published in 2012 by Fox Chapel Publishing Company, Inc. The patterns contained herein are copyrighted by the author. Readers may make copies of these patterns for personal use. The patterns themselves, however, are not to be duplicated for resale or distribution under any circumstances. Any such copying is a violation of copyright law.

ISBN 978-1-56523-726-1

Step-by-step photography by Susan L. Hendrix.

Gallery photography by Jason Anderson.

Library of Congress Cataloging-in-Publication Data

Nish, Dale L., 1932-
Woodturning Christmas ornaments with Dale L. Nish / Dale L. Nish with Susan L. Hendrix.
    p. cm.
Includes index.
ISBN 978-1-56523-726-1
1. Christmas tree ornaments. 2. Turning (Lathe work) I. Hendrix, Susan L. (Susan Laurie), 1952- II. Title.
TT900.C4N57 2012
745.594'12--dc23
                            2012009181

To learn more about the other great books from Fox Chapel Publishing, or to find a retailer near you, call toll-free 800-457-9112 or visit us at *www.FoxChapelPublishing.com*.

We are always looking for talented authors. To submit an idea, please send a brief inquiry to acquisitions@foxchapelpublishing.com.

Printed in China

Fourth printing

About the Authors

DALE L. NISH

For nearly three decades, Dale L. Nish has had a significant impact on the field of woodturning. As an educator, author, and international presenter, Nish has lectured and demonstrated extensively in his travels, making more than 200 national and international presentations at workshops and symposiums. Nish authored the books *Creative Woodturning* (1975), *Artistic Woodturnings* (1980), *Master Woodturners* (1985), and *Woodturning with Ray Allen* (2004). He has also written numerous articles about woodturning and has coauthored several books. In 1982, Nish and his son Darrel started the company Craft Supplies USA, now one of the leading suppliers of woodturning tools and equipment. To learn more, visit *www.woodturnerscatalog.com*.

SUSAN L. HENDRIX

A woodcarver since 1986, Susan L. Hendrix teaches various forms of carving including relief and chip carving and carving in the round. She also teaches classes on woodburning and painting. Hendrix has had several articles published in woodcarving magazines and continues to write. When she moved across the street from Dale L. Nish in 2005, she resumed her interest in woodturning that had began at Brigham Young University in a class taught by Nish. Hoping to incorporate her carving, burning, and painting skills into her turnings, Hendrix took a number of classes at Craft Supplies USA, a company founded by Nish and his son. Hendrix continues to carve and turn while helping coordinate the Utah Woodturning Symposium. She assisted with the writing, editing, and photography of this book.

ACKNOWLEDGMENTS

I would like to thank all my friends and family for their influence in my woodturning experience. Each has made a contribution to my life, and my life has been better for it. Woodturning has enabled me to travel extensively, meet some of the most competent turners in the world, share their experiences, and become good friends with them. My life has been enriched immeasurably. This book is, to a large degree, a culmination of experience and learning with friends and family. I have received support and expertise from all of them. This book could not have been completed without their support. My wife, Norene, was my great encourager, and she also had first choice of the projects I created. I frequently heard, "That's mine," from her.

I would also like to thank the following individuals for their support, technical skill, assistance, and suggestions in the production of this book: Ashley Anderson, Jason Anderson, Don Dafoe, Kristen Gubler, Michael Nish, Darrel Nish, and John Rudert. Also thanks to ten of the best ornament turners I know, as well as other good friends who are identified in the project and gallery sections of the book.

—Dale L. Nish

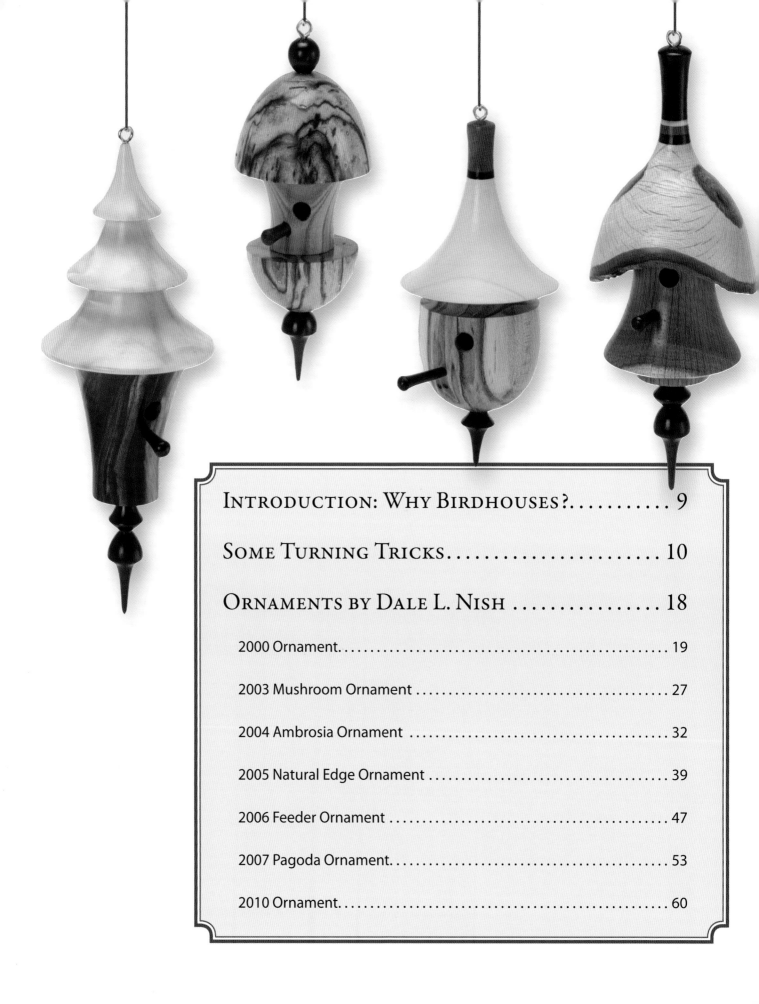

Introduction: Why Birdhouses?........... 9

Some Turning Tricks....................... 10

Ornaments by Dale L. Nish 18

2000 Ornament.. 19

2003 Mushroom Ornament 27

2004 Ambrosia Ornament 32

2005 Natural Edge Ornament 39

2006 Feeder Ornament 47

2007 Pagoda Ornament.. 53

2010 Ornament... 60

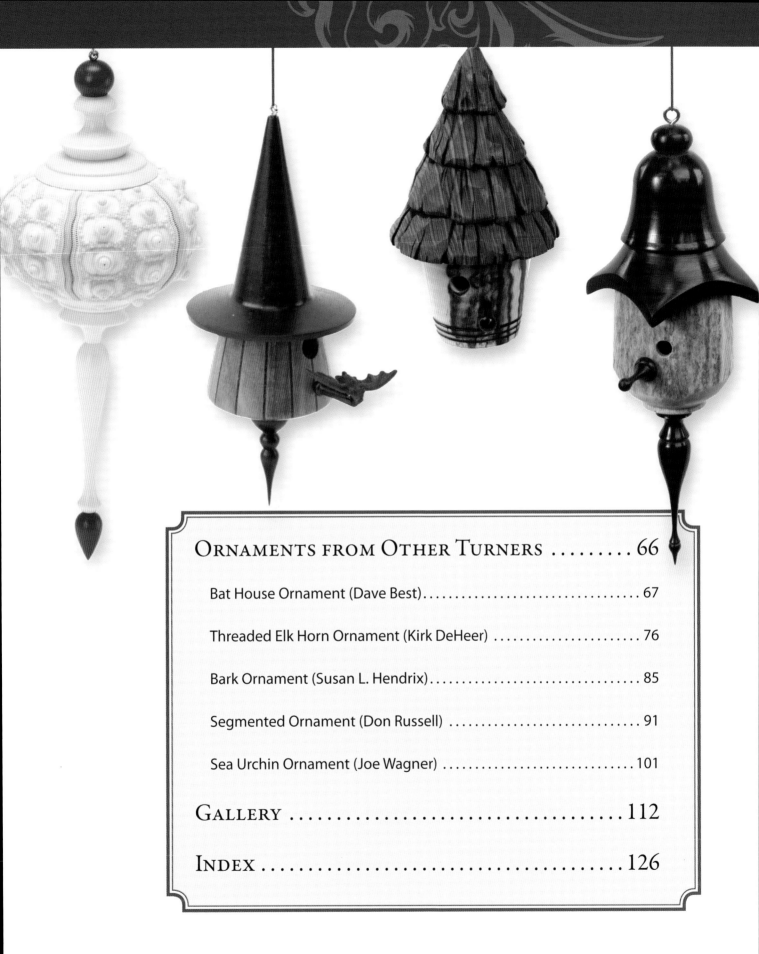

Ornaments from Other Turners 66

Bat House Ornament (Dave Best)................................. 67

Threaded Elk Horn Ornament (Kirk DeHeer) 76

Bark Ornament (Susan L. Hendrix)................................ 85

Segmented Ornament (Don Russell) 91

Sea Urchin Ornament (Joe Wagner) 101

Gallery 112

Index 126

Make Elegant Ornaments for Your Holiday Tree

HERE'S WHAT YOU'LL DISCOVER:

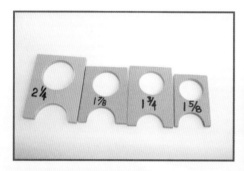

11 How to make useful measuring gauges.

14 How to turn a finial.

17 Tips on finishing.

18 Step-by-step projects from the author.

66 Step-by-step projects from other turners.

112 An inspirational gallery.

Introduction: Why Birdhouses?

Ornaments are popular items to turn because they are fun and challenging projects that require dedication to design and skill to accomplish. They are fun to make, require little material, and the results are gratifying. Birdhouse Christmas Ornaments have become very popular during the last twenty years or so and are treasured gifts to give to family and friends. Since 1993, I have designed and turned birdhouse ornaments for my grandkids, neighbors, family members, and friends, along with some extras to sell at shows or donate to woodturning auctions. I usually turn 50 or more ornaments each year, for a total of 800 to 1,000 birdhouse ornaments since the time I started turning them.

Typically I turn these ornaments in groups of ten or twelve, usually from a variety of colorful or unusual woods. After the bodies and roofs are turned and finished, I match them together, looking for combinations that are interesting or have good contrast or color. I make the perches and finials from dense straight-grained hardwood, typically ebony, blackwood, or pink ivory.

Inside this book, you'll find some of my favorite ornaments from the collection I designed and turned during the past eighteen years. I have also included several extraordinary ornaments turned by some of my friends. You will find five of these ornaments in the second project section of the book, Ornaments from Other Turners (page 66), and you can see even more exceptional work from others in the gallery (page 112).

—Dale L. Nish

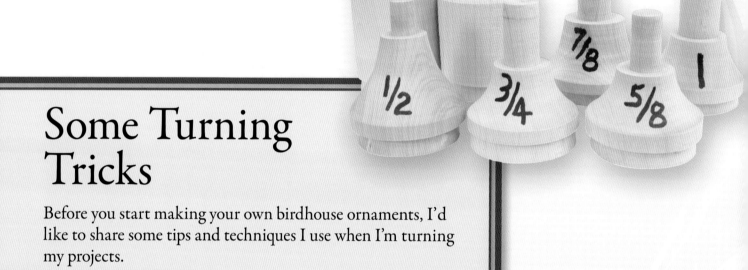

Some Turning Tricks

Before you start making your own birdhouse ornaments, I'd like to share some tips and techniques I use when I'm turning my projects.

TOOLS

The tools I have used in the production of these ornaments are ones that most woodturners have on hand in their workshops. In most cases, you will find you can use the tools you already have to make the cuts necessary to complete the projects. If the tools and materials list calls for a ⅜" (10mm) gouge, and you do not have one, you could easily use a ¼" (6mm) or ½" (13mm) gouge instead. Sometimes specialty tools are required, but often these can be made by shaping existing tools to create the necessary items. Occasionally, you might need to purchase a specialty tool, but this is just an opportunity to add another useful item to your tool rack.

Woodturning requires sharp tools and practice, and practice requires evaluation, or little progress will be made. Keep your tools sharp, practice, evaluate your progress, and have fun!

TEMPLATES

I make and use templates to check the dimensions of cylinders I am turning. I make the templates out of a ¼" (6mm)-thick piece of tempered Masonite. To make your own templates, cut the Masonite into pieces about 3" x 5" (76 x 127mm). Mark a line down the center of each piece. Determine the size of the holes you need to drill based on the size of the drill bits you use most often. I use multi-spur bits ranging in size from ½" (13mm) in diameter to 2¼" (57mm) in diameter. Mark a spot on each Masonite piece to drill a top hole and a bottom hole. Drill holes where you marked them. Now, cut away the bottom portion of the Masonite, so that the bottom hole becomes a half circle (see the photo below). You can use this template to check both the diameter and radius of your cylinders.

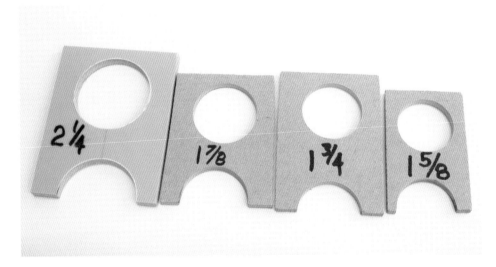

Using templates makes checking the diameter of your projects simple and easy. Make a set like the one shown, including templates for the diameters you turn most often.

MANDRELS

A mandrel is a very useful accessory when turning certain kinds of ornaments. Designed properly, the mandrel's wooden shaft or rod passes into or all the way through the workpiece, holding the drilled piece by the inside surface so the exterior of the ornament can be turned to the desired shape.

Mandrels are usually held in a chuck, which means the end of the mandrel must have a dovetail, but they can also be held by conventional faceplates and screws. A mandrel is typically held on the right side of the headstock and, for greater stability, may be supported by a live revolving center.

Mandrels can be made from most hardwoods, but I prefer close-grained, inexpensive woods such as maple or birch. If you choose to use ash or poplar, however, you will do fine. I also prefer to make mandrels using pieces of wood that are straight-grained and large enough to allow a base diameter of about 2½" (64mm). Pieces this size will fit into most chucks and can be adapted to the best size for the mandrel you need.

To turn a mandrel, start by selecting a piece of hardwood and turning it to a cylinder.

To make a mandrel, turn the hardwood of your choice into a cylinder and cut a dovetail on one end. With this completed, you are ready to turn the working end of the mandrel. Determine the length of the shaft needed to securely seat the drilled blank on the mandrel. A mandrel shaft for the bottom of an ornament will need to be about 1½"–2" (38–51mm) long. The mandrel shaft for the top of an ornament can be shorter, usually ⅝"–1" (16–25mm) long. You can take the rough shaft sizes from the plan for the project you are turning.

Secure the dovetail end of the mandrel in the chuck and turn the shaft to size. Don't make the shaft diameter too small or the mandrel will be unusable. Try placing an ornament body on the mandrel's shaft to check the fit. Turn a small chamfer on the end of the shaft and check the finial dimension. Once the body opening starts to go over the chamfer, the correct diameter of the shaft will be determined. Use the mark on the chamfer as a guide and continue to shape the shaft, removing fine, light shavings and checking the shaft diameter for size. A snug fit with the ornament body is desirable, but not too tight. Holes drilled in different species of wood with the same drill bit can vary in size by several thousandths of an inch, so the mandrel must be turned to fit the smallest hole. If need be, the mandrel's shaft can be padded with masking tape or paper towel to hold body pieces that fit too loosely.

I typically use mandrels with shaft diameters of ½" (13mm), ⅝" (16mm), ¾" (19mm), ⅞" (22mm), and 1" (25mm). The length of the shaft is determined by the requirements of the ornament. I don't put any finish on the mandrels, but simply label them to indicate their size.

Use the project you are creating to determine the necessary length and diameter of the mandrel shaft, and then turn the shaft to those dimensions. Check the fit against the project piece.

If a project piece does not fit snugly on the mandrel, shim the shaft with masking tape or paper towel to get a better fit.

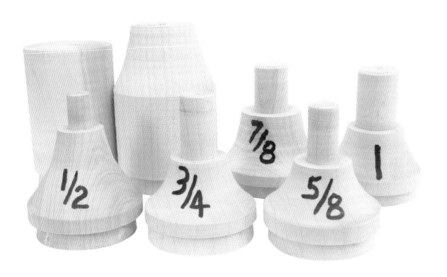

Just like it's useful to have a set of templates, it's also a good idea to have a set of mandrels on hand.

Finials and Perches

A finial is a decorative feature used to accent a point or other structural part of an ornament. Finials can be made using a number of different woods and vary in design and length. A finial has a purely decorative function and is not meant to do anything other than make a striking addition to the design of an ornament. Finials are usually quite fragile and need to be turned from dense hardwoods with little figure or grain pattern. Ebony, blackwood, pink ivory, and holly are excellent woods for making finials.

1 Select the wood. Select a piece of straight-grained wood for your finial. The wood pieces pictured are African blackwood cut from 2" x 2" x 12" (51 x 51 x 305mm) stock. The stock was cut into four pieces, each about 1" (25mm) square. Each of these square pieces can be turned into ¾" (19mm)-diameter dowels or cut again into quarters, yielding pieces about ⅜" (10mm) square. Turning pieces like finials or perches from small stock pieces wastes less material than if larger stock pieces are used. Since the pieces pictured were about 12" (305mm) long, I cut them in half before I started turning. Shorter pieces can be securely held in a chuck with extended jaws.

2 Fit the block in the chuck. Insert the block you have selected about halfway into the extended jaws of the chuck and tighten securely.

3 Round the block. Turn the block into a cylinder.

4 Mark the finial length. Mark the length of the finial on the cylinder, excluding the length of the tenon. I use a set of divider calipers to mark off equal lengths precisely and quickly.

5 Shape the finial. Turn the finial to the shape you desire. Here, I am using a ⅜" (10mm) spindle gouge to shape the finial.

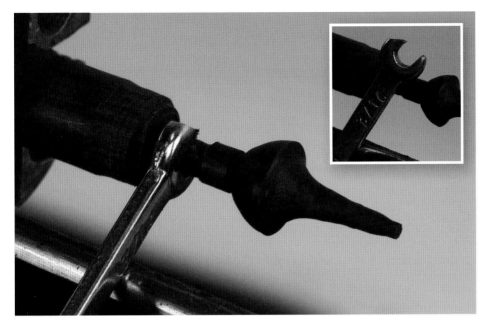

6 Make the tenon. Shape the tenon using your preferred method. I use a ³⁄₁₆" (5mm) wrench ground to a sharp cutting edge on one side to bring the tenon to size. I have a set of open-end ignition wrenches that have been modified as shown for this purpose. Their sizes are ⅛" (3mm), ⁵⁄₃₂" (4mm), ³⁄₁₆" (5mm), ⁷⁄₃₂" (5.5mm), and ¼" (6mm), and these dimensions suit most of my needs.

7 Sand the finial. Sand the finial smooth. I use a hook-and-loop disc power sander with 220-grit and 320-grit discs. Power sanding is very useful, particularly for producing a fine point on the finial.

8 Finish the tenon. Do any necessary final cleanup around the tenon area with a skew in scraping mode. Take paper-thin cuts.

9 Turn a perch and glue in place. Perches are turned using a similar method to the one used to turn the finial. The smaller end of the perch will be ⅛" (3mm) in diameter. Finish your finials and perches using a spray lacquer, and insert them into the bodies of your ornaments. I prefer to use thick cyanoacrylate glue on the inside of the ornament body so it won't show when dry.

Actual Size

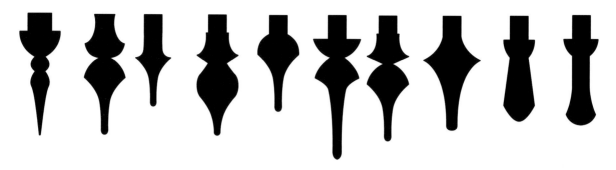

2x Actual Size

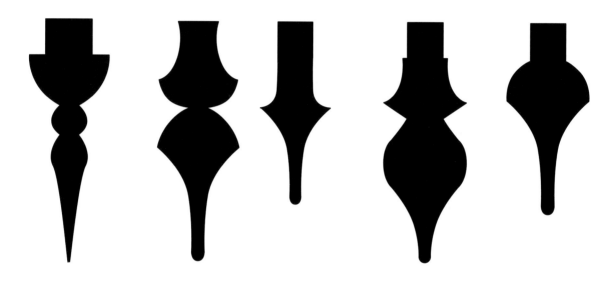

2x Actual Size

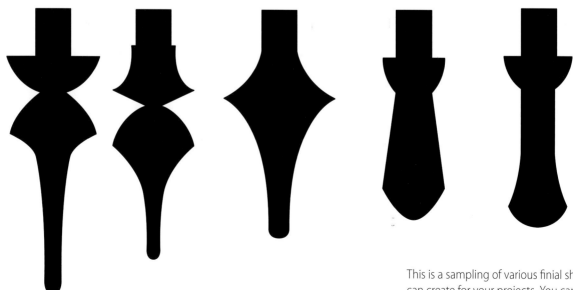

This is a sampling of various finial shapes you can create for your projects. You can also design and turn your own finials.

◆ WOODTURNING CHRISTMAS ORNAMENTS ◆

FINISHING

Use an item like a small Phillips screwdriver or dowel to hold your project piece while you apply finish.

Once you have turned an ornament to shape, the body and roof need to be sanded. I use a power sander with hook-and-loop discs and abrasives and sand the piece using discs with grits 100, 150, 220, 320, and 400 if necessary. Be careful not to over sand the project, making the walls too thin and fragile. Look through the entrance hole and perch hole of the birdhouse to check the wall thickness of the ornament.

I use a sharpened Phillips screwdriver to hold the body and roof of my birdhouse while I spray on the finish. I also constructed a stand from a block of wood drilled with holes large enough to accept the handle of a screwdriver. After spraying on the finish, I place the screwdriver into the stand to allow the piece to dry.

When you are ready to finish your ornament, insert a sharpened Phillips screwdriver into the finial hole in the bottom of the base or body. Alternatively, use a 6" (152mm)-long dowel inserted into the top of the body. Using a screwdriver or dowel will make it easy to hold the ornament while spraying on a full wet coat of lacquer. Use a sanding sealer or gloss lacquer depending on the amount of shine you want the finished ornament to have. If the finish begins to drip, use the holder to rotate the piece until the surface starts to set. Then, set the piece aside until the finish is dry. Depending on humidity and temperature in your area, the lacquer will be ready for a second coat in about fifteen minutes or so. When the finish is dry, put the birdhouse body back on the mandrel and polish it on the lathe with #0000 steel wool and paste wax. Then, buff the piece with a flannel cloth or soft paper towel. Finish the roof using the same method.

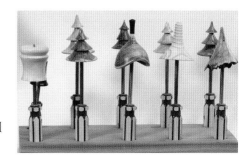

I created this stand so my pieces would have a place to dry while I worked on other projects. You might find a stand like this helpful in your own workshop.

Ornaments by Dale L. Nish

In this section, you will find illustrated step-by-step instructions for creating seven birdhouse ornaments I designed since discovering the concept in 1993. I hope you enjoy making these ornaments as much as I have.

This ornament tree holds a sampling of the numerous birdhouse ornaments author Dale L. Nish has designed and turned. This chapter explains how to make several of them, with detailed step-by-step instructions and accompanying photos.

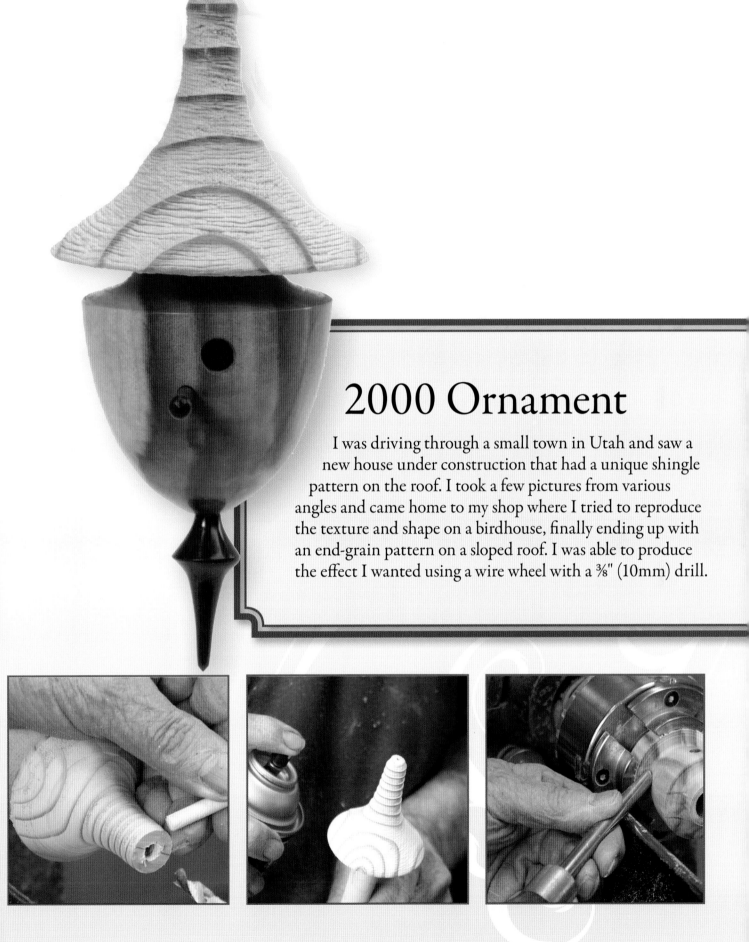

2000 Ornament

I was driving through a small town in Utah and saw a new house under construction that had a unique shingle pattern on the roof. I took a few pictures from various angles and came home to my shop where I tried to reproduce the texture and shape on a birdhouse, finally ending up with an end-grain pattern on a sloped roof. I was able to produce the effect I wanted using a wire wheel with a ⅜" (10mm) drill.

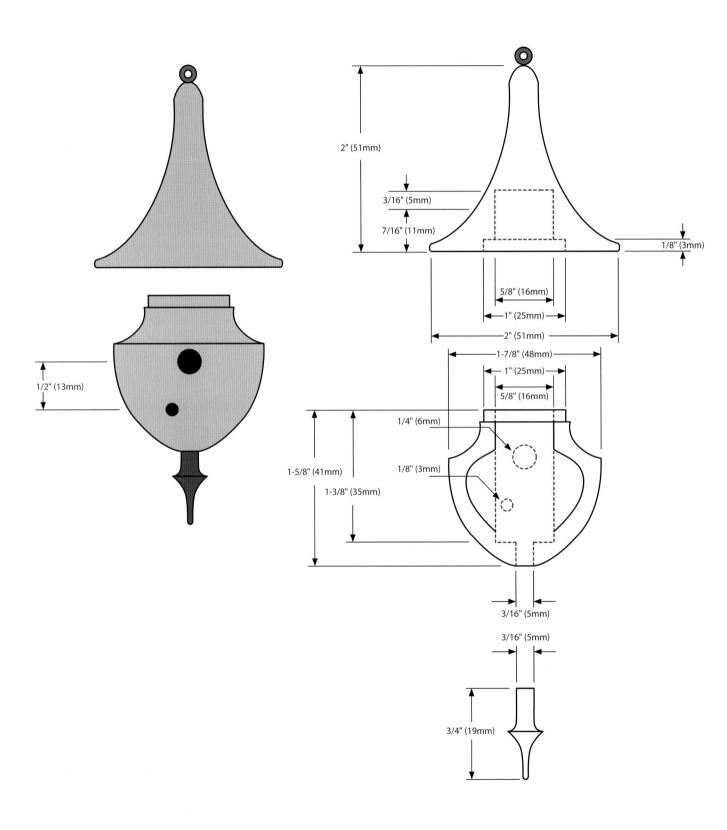

2" (51mm)

3/16" (5mm)

7/16" (11mm)

1/8" (3mm)

5/8" (16mm)

1" (25mm)

2" (51mm)

1-7/8" (48mm)

1" (25mm)

5/8" (16mm)

1/4" (6mm)

1/8" (3mm)

1-5/8" (41mm)

1-3/8" (35mm)

3/16" (5mm)

3/16" (5mm)

3/4" (19mm)

1/2" (13mm)

TURN THE ROOF

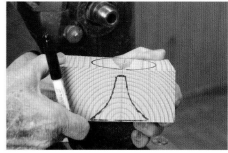

1 **Select the wood.** Select a piece of end-grain fir with the heart center in the middle of the outside surface of the wood as shown. To get the wood pattern desired, you must be able to mark the shape of the roof on the end grain of the wood so the growth rings will be symmetrical on the surface of the roof.

2 **Cut and mark the block.** Cut the block down to about 2⅜" (60mm) wide and 2⅜" (60mm) high. Mark the diameter of the roof as shown.

Tools and Materials

- One 2⅜" x 2⅜" x 2⅜" (60 x 60 x 60mm) piece of end-grain fir (roof)
- One 2" x 2" x 2" (51 x 51 x 51mm) piece of red heart box elder (body)
- One ⅜" x ⅜" x 6" (10 x 10 x 152mm) piece of blackwood (finial and perch)
- Drill bits: ⅛" (3mm), ³⁄₁₆" (5mm), ¼" (6mm)
- Multi-spur bits: ⅝" (16mm), 1" (25mm)
- ½" (13mm) bowl gouge
- ⅜" (10mm) spindle gouge
- Four-jaw chuck
- Four-prong spur center
- Band saw
- Cyanoacrylate glue
- Drill chuck
- Formed scraper
- Parting tool
- Revolving cone center
- hook-and-loop disc power sander
- Sanding discs: grits 100, 150, 220, 320
- Variable-speed drill
- Wire wheel
- Mandrels and templates
- ¼" (6mm) dowel
- Screw eye
- White spray paint
- Spray lacquer of choice
- Black wax
- Soft cloth or rag

The author used these products for the project.
Substitute your choice of brands, tools, and materials as desired.

3 **Round the block.** Mount the block between centers, and turn it to a cylinder.

4 **Turn to the proper diameter.** Using a gouge, turn the cylinder to a diameter of 2⅜" (60mm). Turn a dovetail on the top end of the piece so it will fit into the chuck. Secure the wood in the chuck.

5 **Drill a hole for the body.** Drill a 1" (25mm)-diameter hole ⅛" (3mm) into the cylinder. This will fit over the flange you will make on the top of the body.

6 **Drill a hole for the mandrel.** Drill a ⅝" (16mm)-diameter hole 1" (25mm) into the cylinder. This will fit over the shaft of a mandrel to hold the roof in position for the final turning and sanding.

7 Place the mandrel. Install a ⅝" (16mm) mandrel in a chuck and slide the drilled cylinder onto the shaft. Be sure the fit is tight and the mandrel will hold the cylinder secure for turning and sanding.

8 Shape the roof. Move the cone center into position to help reduce vibration during turning. Turn the roof to shape.

9 Reinforce the roof's top. The top part of the turned roof will be quite weak because of the end-grain wood. Drill a ¼" (6mm) hole about 1" (25mm) deep into the tip of the roof and glue a ¼" (6mm) dowel into the hole. The dowel will reinforce the narrow tip of the roof and provide a secure place for the screw eye.

10 Mark the dowel. Center the dowel inserted in the tip of the roof on the point of the revolving center. This will leave a small mark that will make drilling the hole for the screw eye easier and more accurate.

11 Sand the roof. Sand the roof and do any shaping necessary with a 2" (51mm) hook-and-loop disc power sander. Start with a 100-grit sanding disc, and then finish using discs with grits 150, 220, and 320.

12 Texture the roof. Use a drill with a wire wheel attached to texture the surface of the roof. The wire wheel will remove some of the soft wood and make the growth rings prominent. Use the wheel with a light touch; do not be too aggressive.

13 **Color the roof.** The roof is more interesting if it is colored with white paint, so spray on a wet coat. It will quickly soak into the end grain of the wood.

14 **Buff the roof.** While the paint is still wet, set the lathe to a speed of about 600 rpm. Then, buff the roof with a soft rag. This will remove the paint from the growth rings and they will show as a prominent part of the design. Set the roof aside for a while to dry.

15 **Drill a hole for the screw eye.** Using the mark on the dowel in the roof tip as a guide, drill a hole in the top of the roof large enough to fit a screw eye. The screw eye will be used to hang the ornament.

16 **Lacquer the roof.** Spray the roof with a light coat of lacquer.

Alternative finish. An alternative choice to the white paint used to color the roof is black wax. If desired, buff this into the surface of the wood to give the roof an interesting appearance.

TURN THE BODY

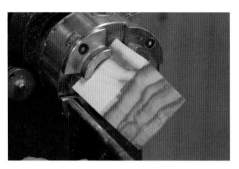

17 **Select the wood.** Select a block of highly figured wood about 2″ x 2″ x 2″ (51 x 51 x 51mm). The piece shown is red heart box elder. Place the wood in a chuck.

18 **Round the block.** Turn the block into a cylinder. I used a ½″ (13mm) bowl gouge, but other gouges work well, too. Select the tool with which you prefer to work.

19 **Measure the cylinder.** Check the dimensions of the cylinder with a 1⅞″ (48mm) template gauge.

20 **Mark the flange and drill the mandrel hole.** Using a 1″ (25mm) drill bit, make a scoring mark on the end of the cylinder. This mark will indicate the size of the flange to be cut later. Then, use a ⅝″ (16mm) bit to drill a hole about 1⅜″ (35mm) deep in the end of the cylinder. Mark a line on the bit so you can tell when you have reached the required depth.

21 **Mark and drill the entrance and perch holes.** Mark the lines for the entrance and perch holes, placing them on the most colorful part of the cylinder. Lock the chuck in position, and drill a ¼″ (6mm) entry hole and a ⅛″ (3mm) perch hole. This is done quite easily with a portable drill; however, if several bodies need to be drilled, a V-block and drill press may be the better choice.

22 Shape the flange and shoulder.

Following the scoring mark for the flange you made during Step 20, use a parting tool to outline the flange on the end of the cylinder. The flange should be 1" (25mm) in diameter and ⅛" (3mm) high. Check the dimensions for fit against the roof piece. Then, use a ⅜" (10mm) spindle gouge and cut a ⅜" (10mm) cove on the shoulder of the body. Try to make the cut clean and smooth so little sanding is necessary.

23 Shape the body.

Use a gouge to remove some of the wood on the outside of the body. Make light, controlled cuts and begin to shape the rounded surface.

24 Hollow out the body.

A formed scraper is used to hollow small, enclosed forms, such as the body for this birdhouse ornament. The hollowing process should leave about ⅛" (3mm) of the drilled hole in the bottom of the piece. This hole is large enough to hold the mandrel's shaft, causing the body to be centered and allowing the final turning and sanding to take place while the wood is held securely. Prior to hollowing out the body, put the formed scraper into the drilled hole and reach down to the bottom. Then, pull the scraper out about ⅛" (3mm) and mark a line. To hollow the body, hold the scraper flat on the tool rest, and make light, scraping cuts from the inside back toward the opening. Frequently blow out the shavings. Continue hollowing until the thickness of the wood around the perch hole is about ⅛" (3mm). Hold a light up to the wood, and look inside the body. The surface should be well turned and smooth. The objective of the hollowing processes is to lighten the ornament so it is easier to hang. Once you have achieved this goal, you can stop hollowing the body.

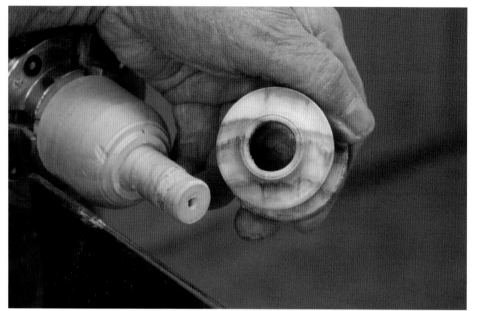

25 **Prepare the mandrel.** After the body is hollowed out, it needs to be placed on a mandrel for the final shaping and sanding. The mandrel's shaft will need to be ⅝" (16mm) in diameter and about 1¾" (44mm) long. The body will slide onto the mandrel more easily if the diameter of the shaft is reduced by ¹⁄₁₆" (2mm) in the center. This will not present a problem when turning the body, as the mandrel will only hold the body at each end, because the center has been hollowed out.

26 **Drill the bottom hole.** Install the mandrel and slide the body onto it. Rotate the assembly and check to see that the unit is running true. Now, insert a ³⁄₁₆" (5mm) drill bit into a drill chuck, and drill a hole through the center of the bottom of the body. This hole will hold the finial.

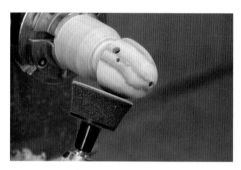

27 **Sand the body.** Use a power sander with a 2" (51mm) hook-and-loop sanding disc to complete the final shaping and remove any tear out or rough pieces. Use a 100-grit disc for the initial shaping and smoothing. When the surface is acceptable, complete the sanding by progressing through discs with grits 150, 220, and 320.

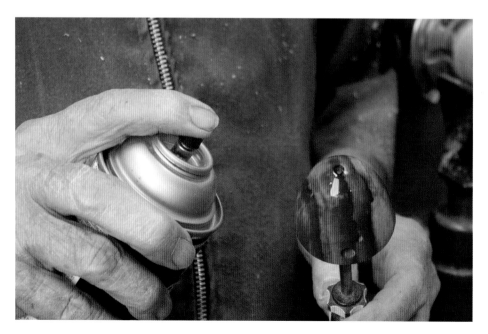

28 **Finish the ornament.** Place the body on a holder and spray it with a lacquer of your choice. I use Masters Magic Sanding Sealer to achieve the finished surface I prefer. Then, turn a finial and perch. Sand and finish and glue them into place. Insert a screw eye.

2003 Mushroom Ornament

Irregular shapes and textures have always fascinated me, and trying to incorporate the shape and surface irregularity of a mushroom into a birdhouse design was a perfect opportunity for me to explore my interests. The organic detail on this ornament was made by using a piece of maple burl for the roof, allowing the natural edge of the wood to outline the roof's edge. I added a little whimsy by using a manzanita twig as a chimney.

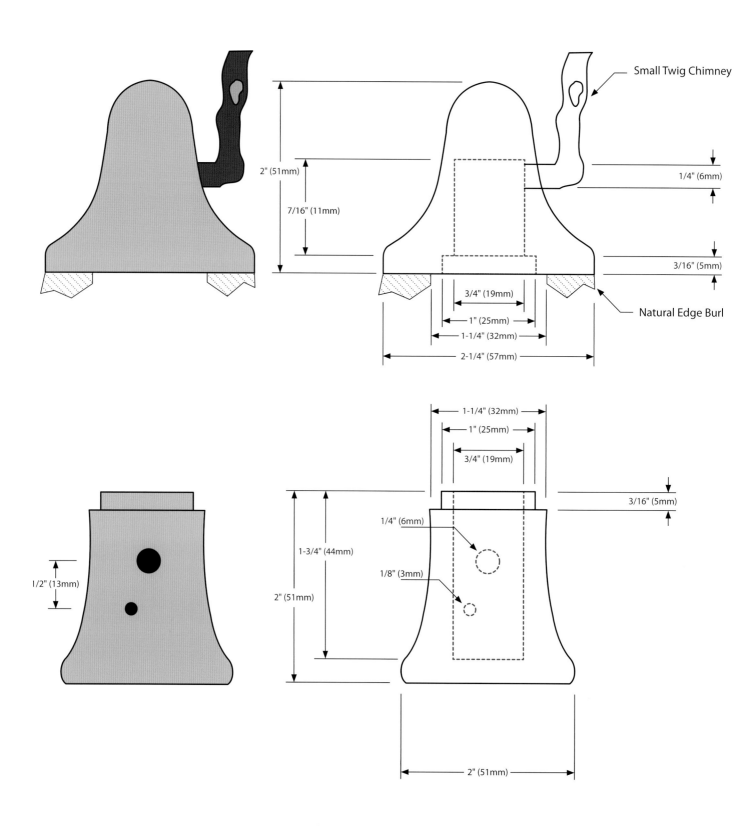

Small Twig Chimney

2" (51mm)

7/16" (11mm)

1/4" (6mm)

3/16" (5mm)

3/4" (19mm)

1" (25mm)

1-1/4" (32mm)

2-1/4" (57mm)

Natural Edge Burl

1-1/4" (32mm)

1" (25mm)

3/4" (19mm)

3/16" (5mm)

1/4" (6mm)

1/8" (3mm)

1-3/4" (44mm)

2" (51mm)

2" (51mm)

1/2" (13mm)

TURN THE ROOF

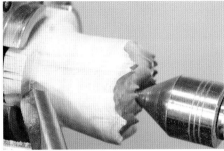

Tools and Materials

- One 2¼" x 2¼" x 2¼" (57 x 57 x 57mm) piece of maple burl (roof)
- One 2⅛" x 2⅛" x 2⅛" (54 x 54 x 54mm) piece of olive (body)
- One ⅜" x ⅜" x 6" (10 x 10 x 152mm) piece of blackwood (finial and perch)
- Drill bits: ⅛" (3mm), ¼" (6mm), 1" (25mm)
- 1¼" (32mm) multi-spur bit
- ½" (13mm) bowl gouge
- ⅜" (10mm) spindle gouge
- Four-jaw chuck
- Band saw
- Center punch
- Drill chuck
- Revolving cone center
- hook-and-loop disc power sander
- Sanding discs: grits 100, 150, 220, 320
- Skew
- Variable-speed drill
- Mandrel
- Manzanita or lilac twigs
- Screw eye
- Spray lacquer of choice
- Cyanoacrylate glue

The author used these products for the project.
Substitute your choice of brands, tools, and materials as desired.

1 Select the wood. Select a block of wood about 2¼" x 2¼" x 2¼" (57 x 57 x 57mm). The block should show a natural surface on one end, such as a rippled or burled surface or the irregular texture left after bark has been peeled off the wood's surface. This surface will form the underside of the roof. The character of a rough surface will add interest to the piece. The photo shows the surface from a maple burl.

2 Round and turn the block. Shape the block using a band saw until it is somewhat round. Then, put it in a chuck and turn the exposed part of the block round to 2" (51mm) in diameter.

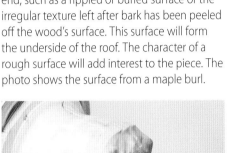

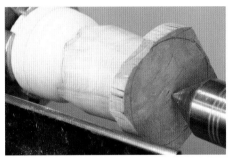

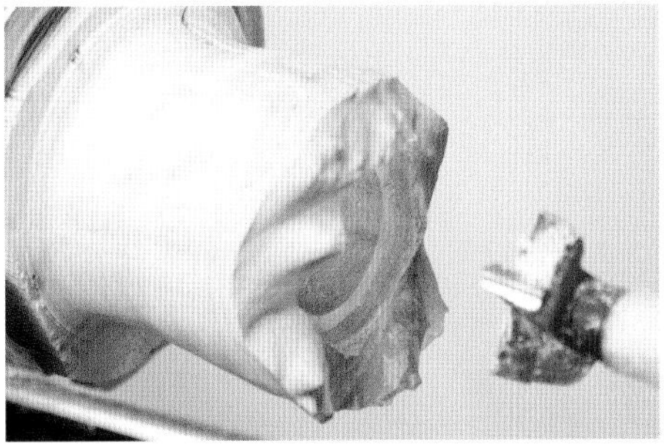

3 Drill holes for the body and mandrel. With the block still in the chuck, use a 1¼" (32mm) bit to drill a 1¼" (32mm) hole about ⅛" (3mm) into the wood. The hole should have a clean shoulder all the way around the surface. The top of the body will fit into this shallow hole. Change to a 1" (25mm) bit and drill another hole inside the first to a depth of 3⁄16" (5mm). Then, change to a ¾" (19mm) bit and drill a hole about 1" (25mm) deep. This hole is for the mandrel and will center the roof and secure it during the final shaping.

4 Place the mandrel. Install a ¾" (19mm) mandrel, and slide the drilled roof block onto the shaft. Move the revolving center into position to help support the roof on the mandrel.

TIP

If you find a piece fits too loosely over the mandrel, put a piece of paper towel over the mandrel's shaft before sliding on the piece. This should shim it enough to make the assembly secure. You can also shim the mandrel with masking tape. One or two wraps is usually all it takes to make the work secure.

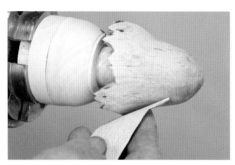

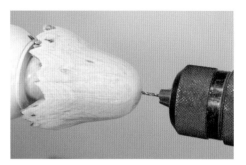

5 **Shape the roof.** Use a ⅜" (10mm) spindle gouge to shape the roof. Make light shearing cuts until you have the shape you want. Don't take off too much wood, or you may expose the drilled hole.

6 **Sand the roof.** Use sandpaper with grits 100, 150, 220, and 320 to sand the roof. Some shaping and the removal of rough patches can be done with the coarsest grit if necessary.

7 **Drill the hole for the screw eye.** Don't remove the roof from the mandrel until this hole is drilled. It is very difficult to get the piece back on the mandrel in the same position it was originally.

TURN THE BODY

8 **Shape and drill the body.** Install a 2⅛" x 2⅛" x 2" (54 x 54 x 51mm) block, and turn it down to 2" (51mm) in diameter as shown. Drill a ¾" (19mm) hole 1¾" (44mm) into the end of the block. Turn a ³⁄₁₆" (5mm) flange as shown; this will fit into the roof. Mark the entrance and perch holes, and then center punch these points. Drill a ¼" (6mm) entry hole and a ⅛" (3mm) perch hole.

9 **Finish the shaping.** Install a ¾" (19mm) mandrel and slide the body onto the shaft. Complete the shaping of the body.

10 **Decorate the bottom.** Use a skew chisel to turn two decorative lines on the bottom of the body. This is also a good place to sign your name.

11 **Sand the body.** Use sandpaper with grits 100, 150, 220, and 320 to sand and smooth the body.

ADD THE FINISHING TOUCHES

12 **Finish the body and roof.** Finish both pieces of the ornament with the finish of your choice. I prefer to use a sanding sealer, as it gives me a good wet coat and dries with a low sheen.

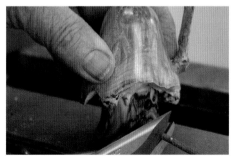

13 **Select twigs for the chimney and perch.** Cut and dry twigs to use for the chimney and perch. The twigs pictured are manzanita and lilac. Try different twigs in different positions until you find the ones you like. Bent twigs make a whimsical chimney, and the crookedness adds interest to the design.

14 **Place the chimney and perch.** Drill a hole for the chimney to fit the diameter of the twig you have selected. The twig does not have to be perfectly vertical unless that is what you want. Glue the chimney twig in place, and cut it to length. Repeat with the perch twig. Insert a screw eye.

2004
Ambrosia Ornament

This ornament has a tapered top, an element I like to incorporate in various ways in my ornament designs. I placed a pink ivory accent at the top of the roof to add color and appeal to the piece. The bulbous shape of the base provides a large area to shape, texture, and color.

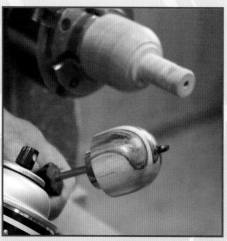

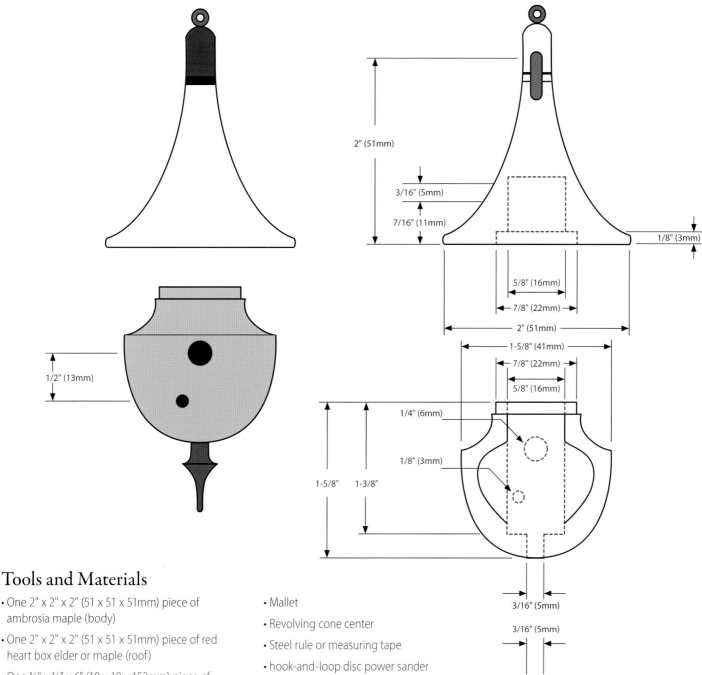

2" (51mm)

3/16" (5mm)

7/16" (11mm)

1/8" (3mm)

5/8" (16mm)

7/8" (22mm)

2" (51mm)

1-5/8" (41mm)

7/8" (22mm)

5/8" (16mm)

1/4" (6mm)

1/8" (3mm)

1-5/8" 1-3/8"

1/2" (13mm)

3/16" (5mm)

3/16" (5mm)

3/4" (19mm)

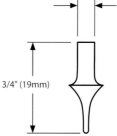

Tools and Materials

- One 2" x 2" x 2" (51 x 51 x 51mm) piece of ambrosia maple (body)
- One 2" x 2" x 2" (51 x 51 x 51mm) piece of red heart box elder or maple (roof)
- One ⅜" x ⅜" x 6" (10 x 10 x 152mm) piece of blackwood (finial and perch)
- Drill bits: ⅛" (3mm), ³⁄₁₆" (5mm), ¼" (6mm)
- Multi-spur bits: ⅝" (16mm), ⅞" (22mm), 1" (25mm)
- ½" (13mm) bowl gouge
- ⅜" (10mm) spindle gouge
- Variable-speed drill
- Calipers
- Drill chuck
- Formed scraper
- Center punch
- Parting tool

- Mallet
- Revolving cone center
- Steel rule or measuring tape
- hook-and-loop disc power sander
- Sanding discs: grits 100, 150, 220, 320
- Four-jaw chuck
- Mandrel
- ⅛" (3mm) dowel
- Cyanoacrylate glue
- Screw eye
- Steel wool
- Wax
- Wood glue
- Spray lacquer of choice
- Soft paper towel

The author used these products for the project.
Substitute your choice of brands, tools, and materials as desired.

TURN THE BODY

1 **Select the wood.** Select a block of wood of your choice about 2" x 2" x 2" (51 x 51 x 51mm). Place it in a chuck or between centers and turn it to round.

2 **Face off the end.** Make a shear, scraping cut across the end of the block to make a flat and true surface.

3 **Cut a groove.** Set your calipers to 1⅝" (41mm), and make a cut with a parting tool to indicate the desired diameter of the block.

4 **Turn to the proper diameter.** Remove wood until the block is 1⅝" (41mm) in diameter.

5 **Round and mark the block.** Reverse the block in the chuck, and remove wood until you have turned a cylinder. Mark lines for the cove, entrance hole, and perch hole at the top of the cylinder. The cove will be about ½" x ½" (13 x 13mm). Mark the entrance and perch holes as indicated on the plan.

6 **Drill and score the body.** Drill a ⅝" (16mm)-diameter hole about 1⅜" (35mm) into the end of the cylinder. Install a ⅞" (22mm)-diameter bit, and make a scoring cut about 1/16" (2mm) deep around the ⅝" (16mm) hole. This scoring line marks the size of the lip that will be left around the hole.

7 **Mark the entrance and perch holes.** Use a center punch to mark the location of the entrance and perch holes. Choose an area with the best figure and color, as these holes will be at the front of the house. The punch marks will also make drilling the holes easier.

8 **Drill the entrance and perch holes.** Rotate the chuck and body so the punch marks for the entrance and perch holes are facing upward. Then, lock the spindle to keep the body from moving during drilling. Drill a ⅛" (3mm)-diameter hole for the perch and a ¼" (6mm)-diameter hole for the entrance.

9 **Turn the cove and sand.** Turn the cove at the top of the body. Then, sand the body using a power sander with a 2" (51mm) hook-and-loop disc. Rotate the body at a normal turning speed while sanding. Progress through sanding discs with grits 100, 150, 220, and 320.

10 **Check the size.** Drill a 1" (25mm)-diameter hole in a scrap block of wood, and use this to check the size of the top of the body. The fit should be snug with about ⅛" (3mm) of the cove entering the drilled hole. This will give plenty of contact for gluing.

11 **Hollow out the body.** Select a formed scraper and hollow out the body. Mark a line on the scraper so that, as the body is hollowed out, about ⅛" (3mm) or more of the original drilled hole is left extending into the bottom of the body. This gives the mandrel a place to center and hold the body true for final turning. As you work, be careful not to enlarge the hole at the top of the body, or the body will not turn true on the mandrel. Take light scraping cuts and remove the shavings frequently, or they may fill the cavity and bind the tool, perhaps breaking the body. Check your work as you go. As mentioned previously, it is critical to leave ⅛" (3mm) or more of the original drilled hole intact. I would argue that it's better to leave too much than not leave enough.

12 **Finish the shaping.** Remove the body from the chuck, and install a ⅝" (16mm) mandrel that has been made to hold the body. Slide the body onto the shaft, and check to be sure it is secure and tight. Move the revolving cone center into position to complete the setup, and then turn the body to shape.

14 Complete the final sanding. Sand the body with a power sander to produce the final shape and a smooth surface. Use a 100-grit sanding disc to remove rough spots and complete any final shaping. When you are satisfied with the shape and surface quality of the body, complete the sanding using discs with grits 150, 220, and 320.

13 Drill the finial hole. With the body still secure on the mandrel, drill a ³⁄₁₆" (5mm)-diameter hole in the bottom to accept the finial.

TURN THE ROOF

15 Finish the body. Place the body on a holder, and spray it with a full wet coat of lacquer. Try to keep the finish from dripping and forming runs, or you will need to sand them out and refinish the piece. Usually two coats of lacquer will produce a good surface finish.

16 Select and shape the wood. Select a 2" x 2" x 2" (51 x 51 x 51mm) block of light-colored wood. Turn it between centers until you have a cylinder. Then, cut a dovetail so it will fit into the jaws of a chuck. Try to keep the finished diameter as close to 2" (51mm) as possible. The dovetail end will be smaller and will be the top of the roof, so the smaller diameter does not matter.

17 Drill a hole for the body. Drill a ⅞" (22mm)-diameter hole about ⅛" (3mm) into the end of the cylinder. This hole will fit over the flange at the top of the body.

18 Drill a hole for the mandrel. Drill a ⅝" (16mm)-diameter hole about 1" (25mm) into the end of the cylinder. This hole will accept the mandrel and hold the roof during the final turning and sanding.

19 **Place the mandrel and roof.** Place a ⅝" (16mm) mandrel in the chuck, and slide the roof cylinder onto the shaft. Use the cone center to support the roof.

20 **Shape the roof.** Begin to shape the roof using a sharp ⅜" (10mm) gouge or another gouge of your choice.

21 **Flatten the top.** Face off the top of the roof, making the area clean and flat.

22 **Add a dowel and top pieces.** Drill a ⅛" (3mm)-diameter hole ¼" (6mm) into the top of the roof. Fit and glue a ¾" (19mm)-long, ⅛" (3mm) dowel into the hole. Then, glue a ¾" x ¾" x ⅛" (19 x 19 x 3mm) feature strip of dark wood with a ⅛" (3mm) hole drilled through it over the dowel. Finally, glue a ¾" x ¾" x ¾" (19 x 19 x 19mm) piece of wood with a ⅛" (3mm)-diameter hole drilled about ¼" (6mm) into it over the dowel as a cap. Gluing the top pieces over the dowel helps strengthen the glue joints, as gluing end-grain pieces together produces weak joints. I like to use Titebond wood glue, but you may use any wood glue of your choice. This glued up assembly must be allowed to dry for three to four hours and preferably overnight.

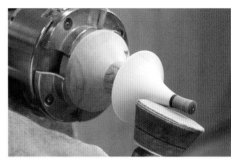

23 **Turn the top of the roof.** Move the cone center into place for support during turning. The point of the center will leave a small indentation in the end of the roof, which makes drilling the hole for the screw eye easier. Turn the top of the roof to its final shape.

24 **Sand the roof.** Use a power sander with a 2" (51mm) hook-and-loop disc to complete the shaping and sanding of the roof. Use a 100-grit disc for the final shaping and then discs with grits 150, 220, and 320 to complete the sanding.

25 **Drill a hole for the screw eye.** While the roof is still in position on the mandrel, drill a hole in the top to hold the screw eye used to hang the ornament.

26 **Finish the ornament.** Spray the roof with one or two coats of lacquer sanding sealer. Let this dry completely. Then, put the roof back on the mandrel, and smooth it with steel wool and wax. Buff with a soft paper towel. Turn a finial and perch. Sand and finish and glue them into place. Insert a screw eye.

2005 Natural Edge Ornament

A bowl with a natural edge inspired the design for this ornament. I have always liked making these bowls, as they can be turned from small, round blocks of wood that still have the bark in place. The bark adds an outline to the piece, creating an effect similar to that of a frame around a picture. The contrast between the brown bark and the white sapwood is very attractive, and the ebony, pink ivory, and holly accent pieces draw your eye to the roof.

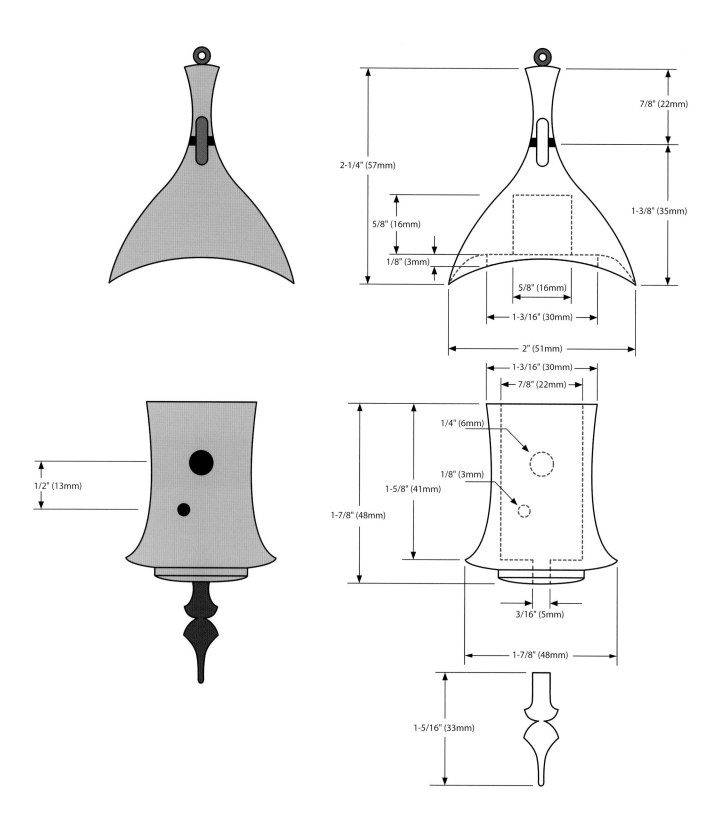

TURN THE ROOF

Tools and Materials

- One 2¼" (57mm)-diameter Gambel oak limb 2½" (64mm) long (roof)
- One ½" x ¾" (13 x 19mm) piece of ebony (roof)
- One piece of holly, ¹⁄₁₆" to ⅛" (0.4 to 3mm) thick (roof)
- One piece of pink ivory, ¹⁄₁₆" to ⅛" (0.4 to 3mm) thick (roof)
- One piece of ebony, ¹⁄₁₆" to ⅛" (0.4 to 3mm) thick (roof)
- One 2" x 2" x 2" (51 x 51 x 51mm) piece of Gambel oak, (body)
- One ⅜" x ⅜" x 6" (10 x 10 x 152mm) piece of blackwood (finial and perch)
- Drill bits: ⅛" (3mm), ³⁄₁₆" (5mm), ¼" (6mm), ⅜" (10mm)
- Multi-spur bits: ⅝" (16mm), ⅞" (22mm), 1³⁄₁₆" (30mm)
- ⅜" (10mm) drive center
- Mallet or hammer
- ⅜" (10mm) spindle gouge

- Four-jaw chuck
- Drill chuck
- Parting tool
- Revolving cone center
- Skew
- hook-and-loop disc power sander
- Sanding discs: grits 100, 150, 220, 320
- Variable-speed drill
- Mandrels and templates
- ⅝" (16mm) dowel holder
- ⅛" (3mm)-diameter dowel, ¾" (19mm) long
- Screw eye
- Spray lacquer of choice
- Soft cloth or rag
- Cyanoacrylate glue
- Wood glue
- Steel wool
- Wax

The author used these products for the project. Substitute your choice of brands, tools, and materials as desired.

1 **Select and drill the wood.** Cut a piece of 2¼" (57mm) limb wood to a length of about 2½" (64mm). Drill a ⅜" (10mm)-diameter hole in the center of one side of the wood to accept a small ⅜" (10mm) drive center. Seat the drive center in the hole, using a hammer to place it securely.

2 **Shape and mark the wood.** Turn the wood until it is egg-shaped. Then, while the wood is turning, mark a line around it about ⅜" (10mm) from the left end.

3 **Check the wood.** Rotate the wood, and compare the distance from the bark on both sides of the wood to the line you drew. If the bark is about the same distance from the line on one side of the wood as it is on the other side, you may continue on the next step. If the line is farther from the bark on one side of the wood than the other, the cone center will need to be shifted so it is splitting the difference between the low side and the high side. To lift the low side, turn the handwheel and allow the cone center's point to reenter the wood at a slightly different place than it did originally. Rotate the wood by hand and note that it is rotating off-center. Start the lathe and make a light cut until the wood is round again. Make another mark at the end of the wood, and check to see if the distance between the line and the bark on each side is nearly the same. If the distance is the same or similar, you have made the proper adjustment and can move on to the next step. If the distance is still drastically different from one side to another, repeat the adjustment process. The low and high sides should be nearly the same to give the roof a balanced look.

4 Cut a dovetail. While the wood is still between centers, turn the end next to the revolving center flat. Then, cut a dovetail on that end, which will fit into the chuck. Place the dovetail in the chuck and tighten securely.

5 Glue the bark. Because every branch has loose bark, run a bead of thin cyanoacrylate glue along the area where the bark contacts the wood. The glue will harden the bark and secure any loose pieces to the wood.

6 Drill a hole for the body. Use a 1³⁄₁₆" (30mm)-diameter bit to drill a hole into the wood. Drill the hole so that it extends about ½" (13mm) into the wood from the low sides of the end.

7 Drill a hole for the mandrel. Use a ⅝" (16mm)-diameter bit to drill a hole about ⅝" into the wood. This will secure the mandrel.

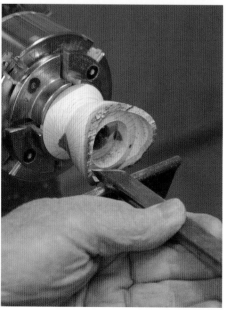

8 Shape the roof walls. Using a skew in a flat scraping position, remove wood around the holes drilled in the end of the wood to create walls about ⅛" (3mm) thick. The walls should extend about ³⁄₁₆" (5mm) beyond the low sides of the roof. This will leave a flat area about ³⁄₁₆" (5mm) wide around the 1³⁄₁₆" (30mm) hole. Blend the shoulders of the walls down to the flat area. If you make clean cuts, this area will not need to be sanded.

9 Glue the edge. Run a bead of thin cyanoacrylate glue around the inside edge of the roof where the bark meets the wood. This will secure any area where the bark may be coming loose.

10 **Place the roof on a mandrel.** Install the roof on a mandrel. Be sure the piece is running true and is tight before you begin turning.

11 **Shape the roof.** Turn the roof to rough shape and face off the tapered area until it is about ½" (13mm) in diameter, flat and true.

12 **Drill a hole for the dowel.** Drill a ⅛" (3mm)-wide hole ¼" (6mm) into the top of the roof. This will hold a ¾" (19mm)-long ⅛" (3mm) dowel.

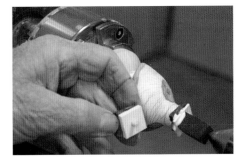

13 **Glue the dowel and top pieces.** Glue the dowel in place. Then, glue on accent pieces of ebony, pink ivory, and holly, capped with a ½" x ¾" (13 x 19mm) piece of ebony. The accent pieces should be ¹⁄₁₆" to ⅛" (2 to 3mm) thick with a ⅛" (3mm)-diameter hole drilled through their centers so they fit over the dowel. The ebony cap should have a ⅛" (3mm) hole drilled ¼" (6mm) into the piece instead of through it. Use the revolving center to center the glued cap piece. Turn the handwheel to put pressure on the glued top pieces. Leave this under pressure for an hour or so. Then, it can be removed from the lathe and set aside. Let the glue set overnight in a warm place.

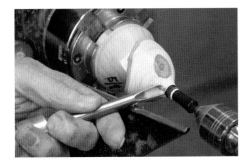

14 **Shape the top pieces.** When the glued top pieces are set, turn the roof to its final shape. Use a ⅜" (10mm) gouge and take light, shearing cuts.

15 **Sand the roof.** Use a power sander to sand the roof. Use a 100-grit sanding disc for any final shaping and the smoothing of tear out or rough patches. Then, use discs with grits 150, 220, and 320 to do the final sanding.

16 **Drill the hole for the screw eye.** While the roof is still in place on the mandrel, drill a hole in the top. This will hold the screw eye used to hang the ornament.

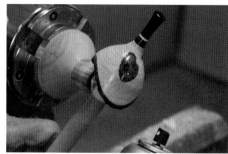

17 **Finish the roof.** Remove the roof from the mandrel. Holding the piece with a ⅝" (16mm) dowel, apply the finish of your choice. Apply two or more coats to get the finish you want.

TURN THE BODY

18 **Select the wood.** Choose a block of 2" x 2" x 2" (51 x 51 x 51mm) wood for the body of the birdhouse. This one pictured is Gambel oak.

19 **Turn to the proper diameter.** Turn the block to a cylinder 1⅞" (48mm) in diameter. Check the measurement with a caliper or gauge.

20 **Flatten and drill the mandrel hole.** Face off the end of the cylinder until it is about 1⅞" (48mm) long, flat and smooth. Using a ⅞" drill bit, drill a hole 1⅝" (41mm) into the end of the cylinder. Mark the drill bit so you will know when you have reached the required depth. This hole will accept the mandrel.

21 **Mark the entrance and perch holes.** Mark the lines for the entrance and perch holes. The lines should go all the way around the cylinder. Choose a figured part of the cylinder and mark center points for the holes. The holes will be at the front of the birdhouse.

22 **Drill the entrance and perch holes.** Lock the spindle holding the chuck, and drill the ¼" (6mm) entrance hole and the ⅛" (3mm) perch hole.

23 **Score and cut the shoulder.** Use a 1³⁄₁₆" (30mm) bit to score a shallow mark on the end of the cylinder, indicating the outside diameter of the shoulder. Use a parting tool to cut a shoulder ⅛" (3mm) high down to the scored line. Use the roof to check the fit. If the shoulder is too large, remove wood until it fits the roof.

24 **Place the mandrel and body.** Install a ⅞" (22mm) mandrel made to hold the body. Slide the body onto the shaft, checking to see that the fit is tight and that the body runs true. If necessary, make a slight adjustment.

25 **Start shaping the body.** Using a ⅜" (10mm) gouge, turn the body to shape, taking light, shearing cuts. Check the plan for shape and size.

26 **Finish shaping the body.** Continue making light cuts to shape the body, leaving a smooth clean surface.

27 **Drill a hole for the finial.** Use a ³⁄₁₆" (5mm) bit to drill a hole in the bottom of the body for the finial.

28 **Round the bottom.** Use a ³⁄₈" (10mm) gouge to round the bottom of the body slightly, forming a curve of about ¹⁄₁₆" (2mm).

29 **Sand and finish the body.** Using a power sander with a 2" (51mm) hook-and-loop disc, complete the shaping of the body and remove any remaining rough spots. Start with a 100-grit sanding disc and continue through discs with grits 150, 220, and 320. Check the work surface carefully, and then blow it clean with an air nozzle. Spray the body with lacquer sanding sealer; it will probably take at least two coats. Smooth the piece using steel wool and wax. Then, buff it for the finishing touch. Turn a finial and perch. Sand and finish and glue them into place. Insert a screw eye.

2006 Feeder Ornament

My wife, Norene, had a bird feeder hanging in our yard. I liked the way the rounded top of the feeder sheltered the feeding table from the rain and snow and allowed the birds to feed from several positions. I decided to make an ornament incorporating this element. The round shape of this piece makes it easy to turn, sand, and finish.

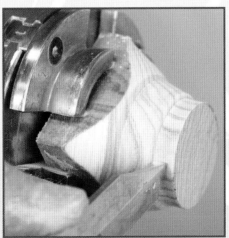

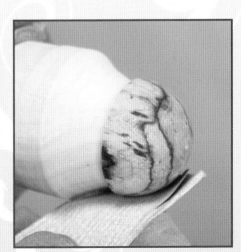

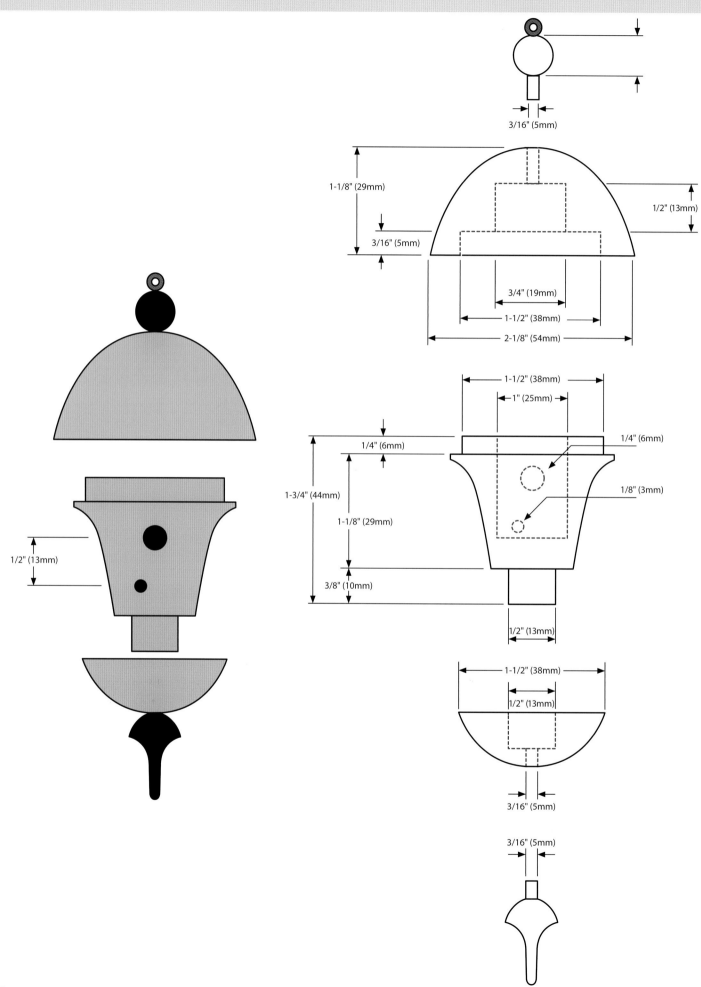

3/16" (5mm)

1-1/8" (29mm)

3/16" (5mm)

1/2" (13mm)

3/4" (19mm)

1-1/2" (38mm)

2-1/8" (54mm)

1-1/2" (38mm)

1" (25mm)

1/4" (6mm)

1/4" (6mm)

1/8" (3mm)

1-3/4" (44mm)

1-1/8" (29mm)

1/2" (13mm)

3/8" (10mm)

1/2" (13mm)

1-1/2" (38mm)

1/2" (13mm)

3/16" (5mm)

3/16" (5mm)

◆ WOODTURNING CHRISTMAS ORNAMENTS ◆

TURN THE ROOF

1 Select the wood. Select a 2" x 2¼" x 2¼" (51 x 57 x 57mm) block of figured wood. Install the block in a chuck or place it between centers on the lathe.

2 Shape the block. Turn the end of the block into a cylinder about 2⅛" (54mm) in diameter.

Tools and Materials

- One 2" x 2¼" x 2¼" (51 x 57 x 57mm) piece of figured black and white ebony (roof)
- One 2" x 2" x 2" (51 x 51 x 51mm) piece of apricot (body)
- One 2" x 2" x 2" (51 x 51 x 51mm) piece of figured black and white ebony (bottom)
- One ⅜" x ⅜" x 6" (10 x 10 x 152mm) piece of blackwood (finial and perch)
- Drill bits: ⅛" (3mm), ³⁄₁₆" (5mm), ¼" (6mm)
- Multi-spur bits: ½" (13mm), ¾" (19mm), 1" (25mm), 1½" (38mm)
- ⅜" (10mm) spindle gouge
- Four-jaw chuck
- ½" (13mm) bowl gouge
- Caliper or ½" (13mm) open-end wrench
- Drill chuck
- Revolving cone center
- Scraper
- hook-and-loop disc power sander
- Sanding discs: grits 100, 150, 220, 320
- Variable-speed drill
- Mandrels
- Screw eye
- Spray lacquer of choice
- Soft paper towel
- Cyanoacrylate glue
- Wood glue
- Steel wool
- Wax

The author used these products for the project.
Substitute your choice of brands, tools, and materials as desired.

3 Flatten the cylinder. Face off the end of the cylinder until it is flat and smooth.

4 Shape the opposite end. Reverse the block and turn the other end until the whole block is a round and clean cylinder.

5 Drill holes for the body and mandrel. Use a 1½" (38mm) multi-spur bit in a drill chuck to drill a hole in the end of the cylinder ⅛" to ³⁄₁₆" (3 to 5mm) deep. This will hold the top of the body. Install a ¾" (19mm) bit and drill a ¾" (19mm)-deep hole in the end of the cylinder. This will accept the mandrel.

6 Install and shape the roof. Place the drilled roof cylinder on a mandrel shaft, and move the revolving center into position to support the block between centers. Turn the roof to shape.

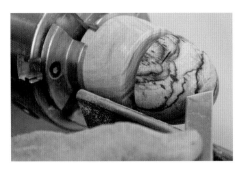

7 **Complete the final shaping.** Use a freshly sharpened scraper to finish the final shaping of the roof.

8 **Sand the roof.** Sand the turned roof starting with 100-grit sandpaper and progressing through grits 150, 220, and 320.

9 **Drill a hole for the screw eye.** While the roof is still on the mandrel, drill a ³⁄₁₆" (5mm) hole in the center of the top. This will eventually accept the tenon of the round ball that will hold the screw eye.

TURN THE BODY

10 **Select the wood.** Select a 2" x 2" x 2" (51 x 51 x 51mm) block of figured wood for the birdhouse body. I usually select a piece that contrasts the color and figure of the roof.

11 **Shape the block.** Turn the block to its rough shape about 1¾" (44mm) in diameter.

12 **Turn a tenon.** Turn a tenon that will fit the 1½" (38mm) recess drilled into the roof. Check to be sure the fit is acceptable. Adjust the tenon diameter as needed until it fits the roof properly. The final fit should be snug but not too tight, as the roof will be glued in place later.

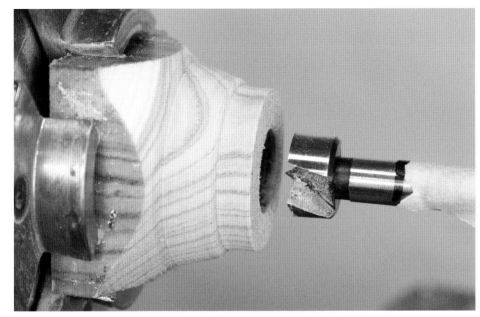

13 **Drill a hole for the mandrel.** Drill a 1" (25mm) hole about 1" (25mm) into the end of the block. This will accept the mandrel.

14 **Taper the body and cut the second tenon.** Remove the drilled block from the chuck. Install a 1" (25mm) mandrel and slide the block onto the shaft. Move the revolving center into position for support and begin to shape the body. First, turn the body to 1¾" (44mm) in diameter and then begin to taper it. When the small end of the taper gets down to about ¹⁵⁄₁₆" (24mm) in diameter, turn a ½" (13mm) tenon using a parting tool. Check the diameter of the tenon with calipers or a ½" (13mm) open-end wrench.

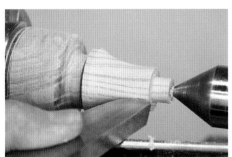

15 **Finish shaping the body.** Use a scraper to slope the body so it has a shallow curve from top to bottom.

16 **Sand the body.** Sand the body, progressing from 100-grit sandpaper through grits 150, 220, and 320.

17 **Mark and drill the entrance and perch holes.** Using the plan for reference, mark the entrance and perch holes. To drill the holes accurately, mark their location with a pencil and then use a center punch to lightly indent the holes. Drill the ¼" (6mm) entrance hole and the ⅛" (3mm) perch hole.

TURN THE BOTTOM

18 **Select and round the wood.** Place a block for the bottom piece in the chuck. Turn one side down to round and then reverse the block. Take the end of the block down to a cylinder 1½" (38mm) in diameter. Drill a ½" (13mm) hole about ½" (13mm) into the end of the cylinder. This hole will hold the body's tenon.

19 **Check the fit.** Check the fit of the body's tenon against the hole you drilled during the previous step.

20 **Flatten and sand the bottom.** Face off the end of the cylinder with a gouge so it is flat and smooth. Sand the surface with all the necessary grits of sandpaper.

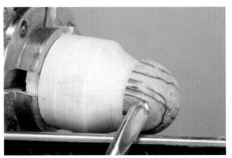

21 **Finish the shaping.** Place the roughed out bottom on a ½" (13mm) mandrel. Using a spindle gouge, complete the shaping. Use light shearing cuts to turn the bottom round and smooth.

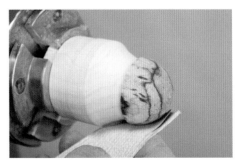

22 **Sand the bottom.** Sand the bottom using sandpaper with grits 100, 150, 220, and 320. Use the 100-grit paper to complete any final shaping as needed.

23 **Finish the ornament.** Spray a full wet coat of lacquer sanding sealer on the bottom. Add additional coats as needed. Smooth with steel wool and wax, and then buff with a soft paper towel. Turn a finial and perch. Sand and finish and glue them into place. Insert a screw eye.

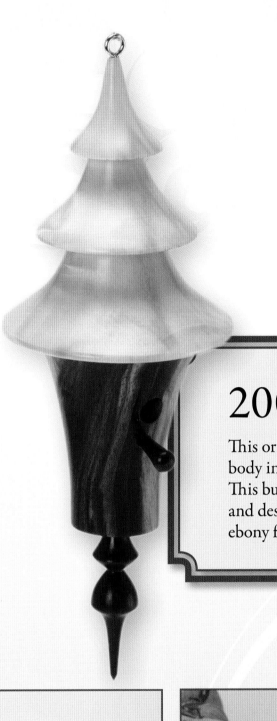

2007 Pagoda Ornament

This ornament uses a Far East pagoda roof and a tapered body in an interesting combination that catches the eye. This building style is seen frequently in Oriental structures and designs. I used figured poplar for the roof and Macassar ebony for the body to give the ornament a pleasing contrast.

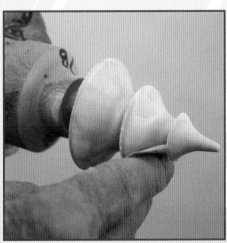

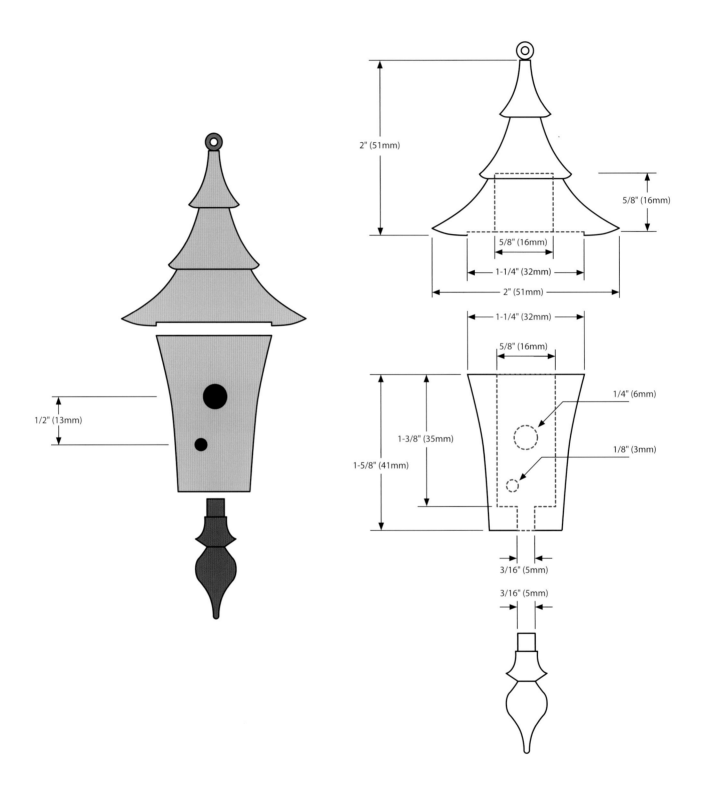

2" (51mm)

5/8" (16mm)

5/8" (16mm)

1-1/4" (32mm)

2" (51mm)

1-1/4" (32mm)

5/8" (16mm)

1/4" (6mm)

1/2" (13mm)

1-3/8" (35mm)

1/8" (3mm)

1-5/8" (41mm)

3/16" (5mm)

3/16" (5mm)

ALTERNATE PLAN

Note the difference in scale between the plan for this ornament and the ornament plan on the previous page.

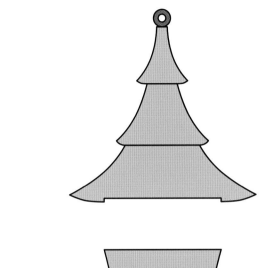

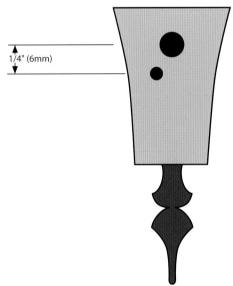

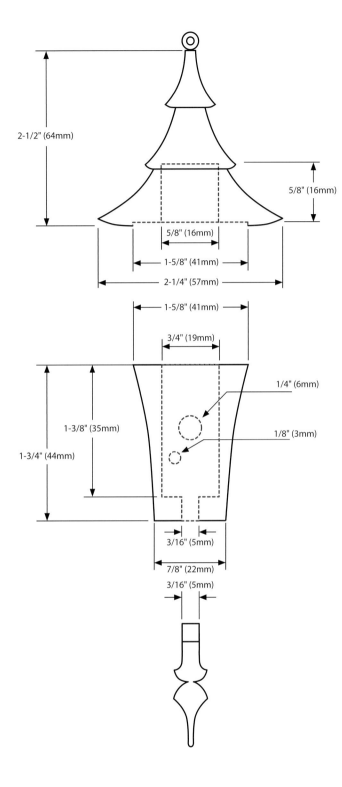

2-1/2" (64mm)

5/8" (16mm)

5/8" (16mm)

1-5/8" (41mm)

2-1/4" (57mm)

1-5/8" (41mm)

3/4" (19mm)

1/4" (6mm)

1/8" (3mm)

1-3/8" (35mm)

1-3/4" (44mm)

3/16" (5mm)

7/8" (22mm)

3/16" (5mm)

1/4" (6mm)

Tools and Materials

- One 2" x 2½" x 2½" (51 x 64 x 64mm) piece of figured poplar (roof)
- One 2" x 2" x 2" (51 x 51 x 51mm) piece of figured wood (body)
- One ⅜" x ⅜" x 6" (10 x 10 x 152mm) piece of blackwood (finial and perch)

- Drill bits: ⅛" (3mm), ³⁄₁₆" (5mm), ¼" (6mm)
- Multi-spur bits: ⅝" (16mm), 1⅝" (41mm)
- ⅜" (10mm) spindle gouge
- ½" (13mm) bowl gouge
- Four-jaw chuck

- Drill chuck
- Revolving cone center
- hook-and-loop disc power sander
- Sanding discs: grits 80, 100, 150, 220, 320
- Variable-speed drill
- Mandrels and templates

- Screw eye
- Spray lacquer of choice
- Soft paper towel
- Masking tape
- Cyanoacrylate glue
- Steel wool
- Wax

The author used these products for the project.
Substitute your choice of brands, tools, and materials as desired.

TURN THE ROOF

1 Select the wood. Choose a 2" x 2½" x 2½" (51 x 64 x 64mm) block of figured wood that will contrast with the wood for the body. I used figured poplar to contrast with a black and white ebony body, but use the combination you prefer.

2 Round the block. Place the block between centers or in a chuck, and turn it to about 2¼" (57mm) in diameter. Check the dimensions with a tape measure or template. Reverse the block in the chuck jaws, and turn it to a cylinder of the proper dimensions. A ½" (13mm) spindle gouge will work well.

3 Drill holes for the body and mandrel. Use a 1⅝" (41mm) bit to drill a hole ¹⁄₁₆" to ⅛" (2 to 3mm) into the cylinder. Then, use a ⅝" (16mm) bit to drill a 1" (25mm)-deep hole. Finally, drill a ⅛" (3mm)-diameter hole ¼" (6mm) into the cylinder. Use this last hole to hold the finished roof with a small screwdriver when applying the finish.

4 Sand the end. Use 220-grit or 320-grit sandpaper to sand the end of the cylinder. This area will form the underside of the roof and will be difficult to sand later.

5 Position the cylinder for turning. Slide the drilled cylinder onto a mandrel, checking that the fit is tight. If necessary, put a layer of masking tape or paper towel around the mandrel's shaft to make the fit more secure. Once the cylinder is in place, move the revolving center into position to support it.

6 Shape the roof. Using a ½" (13mm) spindle gouge, start tapering the cylinder to make a cone shape about ¼" (6mm) in diameter at the small end.

7 **Mark and cut the tiers.** Measure the cone and divide it into three equal parts, marking the divide between each section with a pencil. Then, use a thin parting tool to make cuts about ¼" (6mm) deep along the pencil lines to separate the sections.

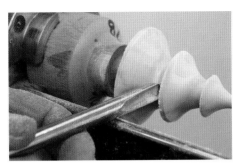

8 **Shape the tiers.** Use a ⅜" (10mm) gouge to remove the wood between the cuts made during the previous step, shaping the cone so it has three tiers. The cuts should be tapered and the surfaces should be cut clean and smooth. Be careful not to damage the tiers as you cut.

9 **Sand the roof.** When the final shape is complete, sand the roof starting with 100-grit sandpaper and progressing to 320-grit sandpaper.

10 **Drill the hole for the screw eye.** Before the roof is taken off the mandrel, drill the hole in the top for the screw eye.

TURN THE BODY

11 **Select and shape the wood.** Choose a 2" x 2" x 2" (51 x 51 x 51mm) block of wood for the body. Install it in a chuck, and turn the end to a cylinder 1⅝" (41mm) in diameter.

12 **Drill a hole for the mandrel.** Use a ⅝" (16mm) bit to drill a hole about 1½" (38mm) into the cylinder.

13 **Mark lines for the entrance and perch holes.** Measure and use a pencil to mark the lines for the perch and entrance holes.

14 **Drill the entrance and perch holes.** Drill a ⅛" (3mm)-diameter perch hole and a ¼" (6mm)-diameter entrance hole. Try to position the holes on the most interesting part of the wood, as they mark the front of the birdhouse. Once you're finished drilling, reverse the block and turn the square end until it is round and you are left with a smooth, clean cylinder.

15 **Shape the body.** Install a ¾" (19mm) mandrel in a chuck and check to see that it is running true. Slide the body cylinder onto the shaft and make sure it is secure. Shape the cylinder in a gentle curve so it is 1⅝" (41mm) in diameter at the top to about 1" (25mm) in diameter at the bottom.

16 **Drill a hole for the finial.** Drill a ³⁄₁₆" (5mm) hole in the bottom of the body to accept the finial after it is turned.

17 **Sand the body.** Sand the body, progressing from 100-grit sandpaper through to 320-grit sandpaper.

FINISH THE ORNAMENT

18 **Lacquer the body and roof.** Spray the body and roof pieces with a lacquer finish of your choice.

19 **Place the finial and perch.** To finish the ornament, turn the perch and finial and glue them in place. Then, glue the roof to the body and insert the screw eye.

2010 Ornament

Cooling towers on a Navajo reservation near Page, Arizona, inspired the shape for the base of this ornament. The shape of the roof is a variation on a tapered point, a design element I often like to include in my work. Ideas for project shapes can be found everywhere—in nature and in ordinary objects like glass, pottery, metal pots and pans, light fixtures, and so forth. Use your imagination!

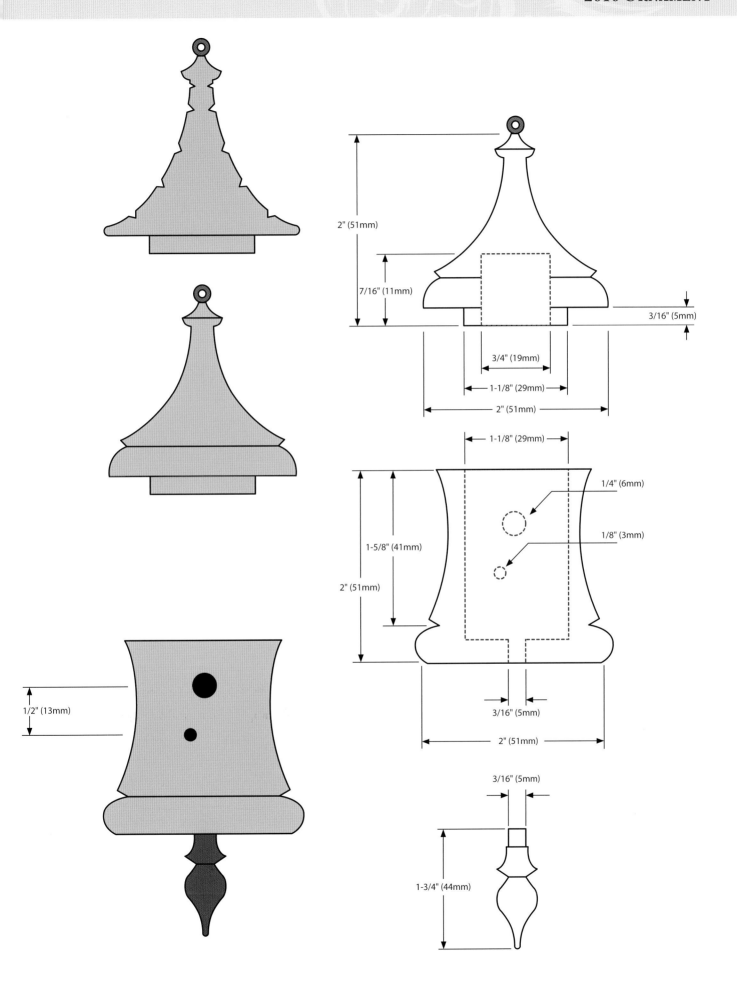

2" (51mm)

7/16" (11mm)

3/16" (5mm)

3/4" (19mm)

1-1/8" (29mm)

2" (51mm)

1-1/8" (29mm)

1/4" (6mm)

1/8" (3mm)

1-5/8" (41mm)

2" (51mm)

3/16" (5mm)

2" (51mm)

1/2" (13mm)

3/16" (5mm)

1-3/4" (44mm)

1 Select and round the wood.
Select a block of wood about 2" x 2" x 2" (51 x 51 x 51mm). Place the wood in a chuck or between centers with the grain running lengthwise, and turn it into a cylinder. If you use a chuck, turn the end of the block to round. Then, lay the gouge on its side, flute toward the block, and face off the end of the cylinder using a pull cut so it is flat and smooth.

2 Turn to the rough dimension.
Reverse the stock in the chuck and turn off the square end. Turn the rest of the cylinder to rough dimension. Check the diameter with a gauge or with your calipers. It should be about 2" (51mm), plus or minus 1/8" (3mm) or so.

Tools and Materials

- One piece of goncalo alves slightly larger than 2" x 2" x 2" (51 x 51 x 51mm) (roof)
- One 2" x 2" x 2" (51 x 51 x 51mm) piece of holly (body)
- One 3/8" x 3/8" x 6" (10 x 10 x 152mm) piece of blackwood (finial and perch)
- Drill bits: 1/8" (3mm), 3/16" (5mm), 1/4" (6mm), 3/4" (19mm)
- 1 1/8" (29mm) multi-spur bit
- 3/8" (10mm) spindle gouge
- Four-jaw chuck
- Calipers
- Center punch
- Drill chuck
- Parting tool/skew
- Revolving cone center
- hook-and-loop disc power sander
- Sanding discs: grits 100, 150, 220, 320
- Variable-speed drill
- Mandrels and templates
- Screw eye
- Spray lacquer of choice
- Soft paper towel
- Cyanoacrylate glue
- Steel wool
- Wax

The author used these products for the project.
Substitute your choice of brands, tools, and materials as desired.

3 Drill a hole for the mandrel. Take a 1 1/8" (29mm)-diameter multi-spur bit and mark the shaft 1 5/8" (41mm) from the end of the bit with a piece of masking tape or magic marker. Reduce the lathe speed to 750 rpm and drill a 1 5/8" (41mm)-deep hole into the cylinder.

4 Mark lines for the entrance and perch holes. Using the plan for reference, mark lines for the entrance and perch holes. Center punch the holes for easy drilling, making sure to place them on the most interesting area of the wood.

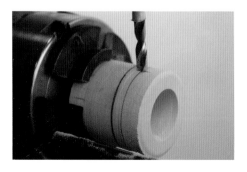

5 Drill the entrance and perch holes.
Drill a 1/4" (6mm)-diameter entrance hole and a 1/8" (3mm)-diameter perch hole.

6 Secure the mandrel and body.
Secure a mandrel in place and slide the body cylinder onto the shaft.

7 Drill a hole for the finial. Drill a ³⁄₁₆" (5mm)-diameter hole in the bottom of the cylinder for the finial. This hole will also act as a center point for the cone center.

8 Turn the first bead and shape the bottom. Using the plan for reference, mark and cut the bottom bead, holding the finished diameter to 2" (51mm). Cut a partial bead to determine the width, but don't cut to full depth yet. Then, use a ³⁄₈" (10mm) gouge and make a cut across the bottom of the body to create a concave surface about ¹⁄₁₆" (2mm) deep.

9 Adjust the diameter. Reduce the rest of the body to a diameter of 1⁵⁄₈" (41mm) at the top end. Check the measurement with a 1⁵⁄₈" (41mm) template or calipers.

10 Finish shaping the body. Turn a radius on the center of the body. A gentle curve will reduce the thickness of the wall at the entrance hole to ⅛" (3mm).

11 Sand the body. Sand the body, starting with 100-grit sandpaper and then progressing through grits 150, 220, and 320.

12 Finish the body. Use a spray lacquer of your choice to finish the body. Set aside to dry.

TURN THE ROOF

13 **Select and shape the wood.** Select a block of wood a little larger than 2" x 2" x 2" (51 x 51 x 51mm). Turn it between centers until it is 2" (51mm) in diameter and about 2" (51mm) long. You may also place the piece in a chuck and turn one end to this diameter.

14 **Shape the other end.** If you used a chuck for the previous step, reverse the block and round the opposite end until you have a cylinder.

15 **Drill holes for the body and mandrel.** Slow the lathe speed to about 700 rpm and use a 1⅛" (29mm) multi-spur bit to score a mark on the end of the cylinder. This mark indicates the outside diameter of the shoulder that will be cut on the bottom of the roof. Install a ¾" (19mm) bit and drill a hole about 1" (25mm) deep into the cylinder for the mandrel. Finally, drill a ⅛" (3mm) hole ½" (13mm) into the cylinder to accept the holder used when finishing the piece.

16 **Cut the shoulder.** Cut a ⅛" (3mm) shoulder on the end of the cylinder using the scored mark as a guide. Use a parting tool or skew chisel to make this cut.

17 **Check the fit.** Use the body turned previously to check the size of the roof's shoulder.

18 **Position a mandrel and the roof cylinder.** Secure a mandrel in place and slide the roof cylinder onto the shaft. If the fit is a little loose, place a piece of paper towel or masking tape around the shaft to produce a tight fit.

19 **Shape the roof.** Use a ⅜" (10mm) spindle gouge to shape the roof, following the plan. Once you have finished, remove the cone center and use a narrow parting tool to part off the roof. Remove the cone center and replace it with a chuck and small drill bit.

20 **Drill a hole for the screw eye.** While the roof is still in place, drill a hole in the end to fit the screw eye.

21 **Sand the roof.** Sand the roof starting with 100-grit sandpaper and progressing through grits 150, 220, and 320.

22 **Finish the ornament.** Spray the roof with a lacquer finish of your choice. Smooth it with steel wool and wax and polish the finished piece with a soft paper towel. Then, turn a finial and perch. Sand and finish and glue them into place. Insert a screw eye.

Ornaments from Other Turners

In this section, you will find illustrated step-by-step instructions for creating five additional Christmas ornaments. These ornaments have been designed by some great turners and will make a wonderful addition to your tree.

Bat House Ornament

My wife loves Halloween and requested I make her some ornaments specifically for that holiday. I felt the Halloween ornaments should not only match the traditional character of Halloween, but also fit the fall season. I decided to make a series of ornaments that incorporated bat houses, witch hats, pumpkins, butternut squash, and acorns, as well as basic geometric shapes. The body of this ornament is made of thirteen (an unlucky, Halloween-type number) segments of chakte viga—selected for its natural orange color—and thirteen pieces of veneer, dyed black. The witch's hat that forms the roof is Gaboon ebony, as are the perch and finial.

Designed and turned by Dave Best. See more of Dave's work in the gallery section on page 113.

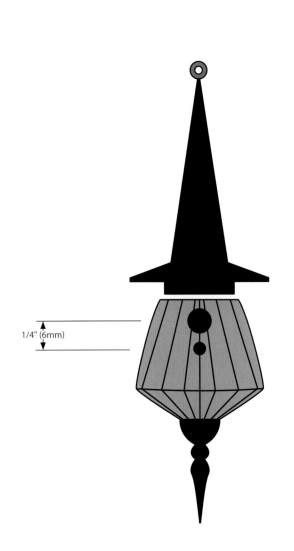

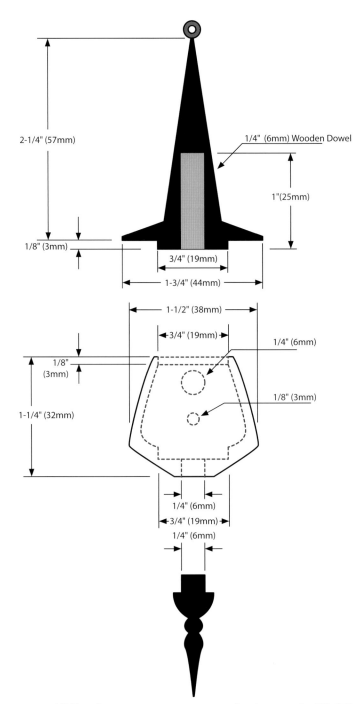

1/4" (6mm)

2-1/4" (57mm)

1/8" (3mm)

1/4" (6mm) Wooden Dowel

1"(25mm)

3/4" (19mm)

1-3/4" (44mm)

1-1/2" (38mm)

3/4" (19mm)

1/4" (6mm)

1/8"
(3mm)

1/8" (3mm)

1-1/4" (32mm)

1/4" (6mm)

3/4" (19mm)

1/4" (6mm)

Tools and Materials

- 13 wedges of wood large enough to form a cylinder 1½" (38mm) tall and 1½" to 2" (38 to 51mm) in diameter (body)
- 13 thin veneer pieces (body)
- 2 pieces of ebony, glued together, large enough to form a piece 2¼" (57mm) tall, 1¾" (44mm) in diameter (roof)
- One ½" x ½" x 5" (13 x 13 x 127mm) piece of blackwood or ebony (finial)

- One ½" x ½" x 5" (13 x 13 x 127mm) piece of blackwood or ebony (perch)
- Drill bits: ⅛" (3mm), ¼" (6mm)
- ¾" (19mm) multi-spur bit
- ½" (13mm) bowl gouge
- ¼" (6mm) open-end wrench
- Calipers or ⅛" (3mm) open-end wrench
- Steb drive center

- ¼" (6mm) cup center
- Small, round nose scraper
- Modified gouge scraper
- ⅜" (10mm) round skew chisel
- Drill chuck
- Parting tool
- Revolving cone center
- Steel rule or measuring tape
- Four-jaw chuck
- Extended-jaw chuck

- Sandpaper: grits 100, 150, 220, 320, 400
- ¼" (6mm) dowel
- Screw eye
- Synthetic steel wool
- Thin cyanoacrylate glue
- Wood glue
- Lacquer of choice
- Soft paper towel
- Woodburner with writing tip

The author used these products for the project.
Substitute your choice of brands, tools, and materials as desired.

TURN THE BODY

1 **Make the body blank.** To start, cut thirteen wedges that each have a 13.8° angle. Glue them together with a thin piece of veneer between each one to form a rough cylinder that is about 1½" (38mm) in diameter and 1½" to 2" tall (38 to 51mm). Construct a sled like the one pictured to help cut the wedges.

2 **Smooth the blank.** Position the body blank between centers. Dave is using a steb center to drive the base. Use a gouge to turn the blank until it is round and smooth.

3 **Mark the entrance and perch holes and cut a tenon.** Dave has several templates he uses to mark the perch and entrance holes on his ornaments, depending on the design. Each template is fitted with sharp nails. By holding the template against the body, Dave scores lines indicating where to drill the holes. You can use Dave's method or mark the perch and entrance holes using a pencil. Once you've finished, cut a tenon on the bottom (tailstock end) of the blank to grip in the chuck.

4 **Drill the entrance and perch holes.** Drill a ⅛" (3mm) perch hole and a ¼" (6mm) entrance hole along the lines marked previously.

5 **Drill a hole for the body cavity.** Install a ¾" (19mm) bit in the drill chuck and drill a hole ¾" (19mm) into the blank.

6 **Hollow out the blank.** Use a small round nose scraper to hollow out a cavity inside the blank. Be careful that you don't remove too much wood and make the walls too thin. Then, place a ¾" (19mm) bit into the cavity and drill a ¼" (6mm)-deep hole. This will hold the mandrel during the shaping of the body.

7 **Select a mandrel.** Dave uses a shop-made expanding mandrel for his ornaments. To use this type of mandrel, slide your workpiece over the mandrel body and tighten the screw at the rear of the mandrel body to hold the wood in place. You can also choose to use a standard mandrel.

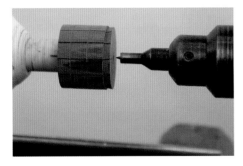

8 **Position the mandrel and body blank.** If you choose to use an expanding mandrel, slide the body blank onto the mandrel's shaft before securing the mandrel on the lathe spindle. Then, expand the mandrel until the body piece is secure. Secure the complete unit on the lathe spindle.

9 **Shape the bottom.** Using a modified gouge scraper, take shearing cuts to shape the bottom of the body.

10 **Taper the body.** Make shaping cuts, tapering the body toward the top of the piece.

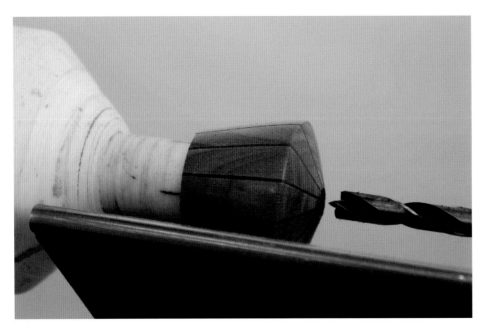

11 **Drill a hole for the finial.** With the body still on the lathe, drill a ¼" (6mm) hole in the bottom to accept a finial.

12 Sand the body. Sand the body, starting with 100-grit sandpaper and progressing through 400-grit sandpaper.

13 Polish the body. Smooth the surface of the body even further by polishing it with steel wool.

14 Finish the body. Apply a wet coat of lacquer of your choice to the body and then wipe the piece with a soft paper towel.

15 Buff the body. Buff the body dry with the lathe running at about 800 rpm.

TURN THE ROOF

16 Make the roof blank. Make the blank for the roof of the bat house by gluing together two pieces of ebony as shown, using a ¼" x 1" (6 x 25mm) dowel to reinforce the joint. Ebony is quite expensive, and creating the blank this way saves a great deal of wood.

17 Shape the roof. Place the roof blank in a chuck, and turn the long thin piece to a smooth, flat surface. Then, reverse the blank and put it back in the chuck.

18 **Cut a tenon.** Turn a tenon that is ¾" (19mm) in diameter and about ⅛" (3mm) on the base of the roof. This is used to secure the roof to the body and also allows the roof to be reversed and held in the chuck while the top of the roof is turned. Use a parting tool to cut the tenon and an open-end wrench to check the diameter.

19 **Check the fit.** Use the body of the house to check the fit of the tenon. Notice that the underside of the roof is slightly undercut.

20 **Finish the roof base.** Use a gouge to true up the base of the roof, making it round and bringing it to the proper dimension.

21 **Smooth the roof base.** Sand the turned area and smooth it using steel wool.

22 **Sign and finish your work.** Sign your name on the base of the roof by using a hot wire to singe the wood. You will want to sign your name or write a message now, as it will be difficult to sign the roof when the ornament is assembled. After signing, apply lacquer to the base of the roof, wipe it dry, and polish it using the same method you did for the body piece.

23 **Shape the top of the roof.** With the long thin portion of the roof still held in the chuck, begin to shape the top side of the roof.

24 **Reposition the roof.** Modify the chuck so it will firmly grip the short tenon on the base of the roof. If this is not practical, make the tenon longer so it can be placed in a standard chuck. Move the tailstock so the revolving cone center will contact the center of the cylinder and help hold the roof securely while the shaping is completed.

25 **Finish shaping the top of the roof.** Take light cuts, gradually tapering the roof. Do not, however, remove the nub holding the center point.

26 **Sand and polish the top of the roof.** When the tapered area is flat and true, sand and polish the turned area.

27 **Shape the roof tip.** Move the revolving center and tailstock out of the way and take light cuts to remove the remainder of the nub at the tip of the roof.

28 **Finish and mark the roof tip.** Sand and polish the tip of the roof. Then, while the roof is still in place in the chuck, use the long point of a skew chisel to make an entry point on the tip of the roof.

29 **Drill a hole for the screw eye and finish.** Using the skew mark to help guide the bit, drill a hole in the roof tip to accept a screw eye. Insert the screw eye, adding a drop of super glue to hold it in place if necessary. Apply lacquer, wipe dry, and polish.

TURN THE PERCH AND FINIAL

30 **Select and round the wood.** Select a ½" x ½" x 5" (13 x 13 x 127mm) piece of ebony. Secure one end in a chuck (an extended-jaw chuck works well) and move the revolving center into position to support the other end of the stock. Turn the entire square to round.

31 **Shape the finial.** Turn the finial to the shape in the plan or turn your own design. Sand the finial after you have finished shaping it.

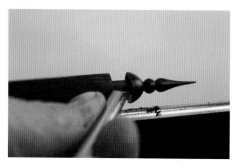

32 **Cut a tenon.** Cut a tenon at the top of the finial to fit the hole in the base of the body. Make the tenon ¼" to ⅜" (6 to 10mm) long.

33 **Finish the finial.** Give the finial a coat of lacquer and wipe it. Then, buff it dry. Finally, part off the finial and set it aside.

34 **Select and round the wood.** Select a round or square piece of ebony approximately ½" x ½" x 5" (13 x 13 x 127mm). Secure it in the long jaws of a chuck and turn it down to the desired diameter.

35 **Finish the perch.** Turn the perch to its final shape. Sand, lacquer, and polish the wood. Shape a ⅛" (3mm) tenon at the back of the perch to fit the hole drilled into the body. Check the diameter of the tenon with calipers or an open-end wrench.

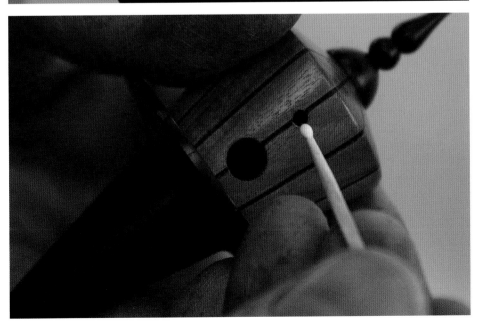

36 **Glue the perch and finial in place.** Use white glue to glue the perch and finial in place. Glue a bat on the perch if desired. Bats may be purchased at your local craft store.

Threaded Elk Horn Ornament

Having Dale L. Nish as friend and mentor, I have been interested in birdhouse ornaments for many years. The ornament presented here reflects my preference for using unusual materials, thread chasing, and turning square rims. The basic design of this ornament takes inspiration from some of the ornaments Dale has created over the years.

Designed and turned by Kirk DeHeer. See more of Kirk's work in the gallery section on page 116.

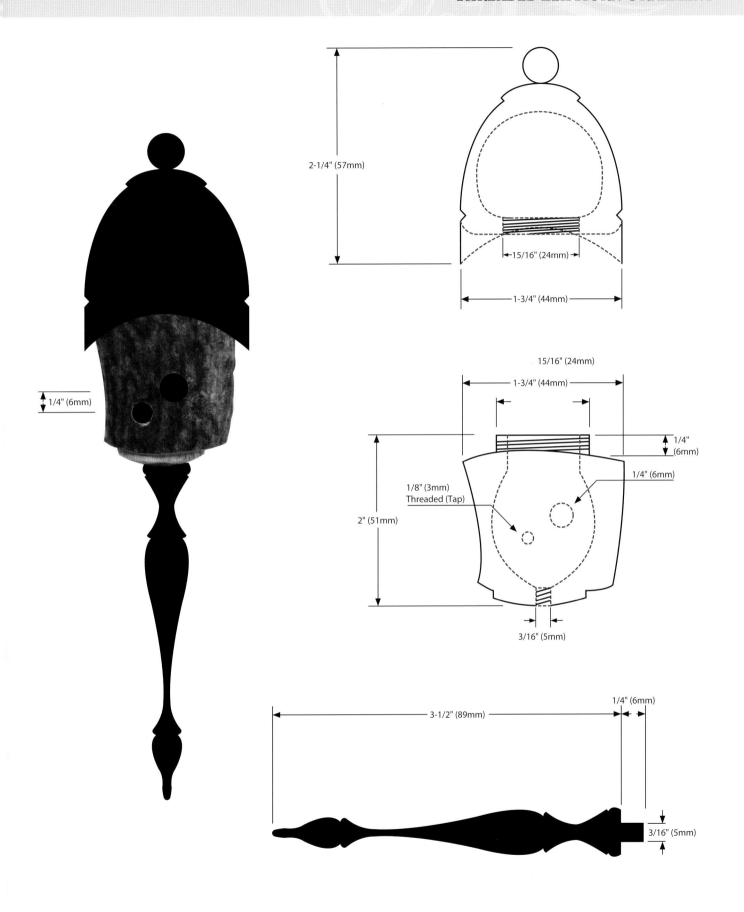

2-1/4" (57mm)

15/16" (24mm)

1-3/4" (44mm)

1/4" (6mm)

15/16" (24mm)

1-3/4" (44mm)

1/4" (6mm)

1/4" (6mm)

1/8" (3mm)
Threaded (Tap)

2" (51mm)

3/16" (5mm)

3-1/2" (89mm)

1/4" (6mm)

3/16" (5mm)

TURN AND THREAD
THE ROOF

1 **Select the wood.** Select a block of 1½" x 1½" x 2" (38 x 38 x 51mm) ebony or blackwood. Mount it between centers, using a small cup revolving center.

Tools and Materials

- One 1½" x 1½" x 2" (38 x 38 x 51mm) piece of ebony or blackwood (roof)
- One 1¼" x 2" x 2" (32 x 51 x 51mm) piece of elk horn (body)
- One ¾" x ¾" x 4" (19 x 19 x 102mm) piece of ebony (finial)
- One 1" x 1" x 1½" (25 x 25 x 38mm) piece of ebony (perch)
- ¼" (6mm) drill bit
- #7 drill bit
- ⅜" (10mm) spindle gouge
- Four-jaw chuck
- Drill chuck
- Heavy parting tool
- Round-nose chisel with reverse bevel
- Negative rake modified scraper
- ¼" (6mm) square-point scraper
- Keyless chuck
- Skew
- Steb drive center
- Formed scraper
- ¼" (6mm) cup revolving center
- ⁵⁄₁₆" (8mm)-diameter threading tool, 20 TPI
- ¼" (6mm)-20 tap
- Beading tool
- Extended-jaw chuck
- Sandpaper: grits 100, 150, 220, 320, 400, 600
- Variable-speed drill
- Screw eye
- Friction polish
- Renaissance wax
- Spray lacquer of choice
- Cloth or soft paper towel
- Thin cyanoacrylate glue
- ¼" (6mm) turquoise cabochon

The author used these products for the project.
Substitute your choice of brands, tools, and materials as desired.

2 **Cut a tenon.** Round one end of the block with a heavy parting tool, forming a tenon about ¼" (6mm) long.

3 **Place the block in a chuck.** Reverse the block and install the tenon in a chuck. Move the revolving center into position at the end of the block, making the block secure for further turning.

4 **Shape the roof.** Remove some wood from the block and begin to shape the outside of the roof. Be sure to leave a flat area as shown. Also start to turn the end of the block to a concave shape, beginning to form the recess of the roof.

5 **Shape and hollow the roof bottom.** Remove the live center to provide the necessary space to shape the inside of the roof. (Use the plan for reference.) Using a round-nose chisel with a negative rake bevel, scrape across the inside of the roof's recess to get a smooth surface. Turn or drill a ⅞" (22mm) hole about ¾" (19mm) into the end of the block, creating a space for the thread.

6 Make a relief cut. Make a relief cut in the bottom of the hole hollowed during the previous step prior to threading. The space is necessary to prevent the thread chaser from bottoming out. The rim of the hole should have straight sides and be clean and smooth.

7 Cut the threads. Cut the threads inside the hole using a thread chaser. Leaving the roof in the chuck, remove the whole unit from the lathe and set it aside.

TURN AND THREAD THE BODY

8 Select the antler. Select a piece of antler about ¼" (6mm) larger in diameter than the hole in the roof and about 2" (51mm) long. The piece pictured is a piece of elk antler 1¼" (32mm) in diameter and 2" (51mm) long.

9 Cut a tenon. Turn the antler between centers and square off the ends. Turn a tenon on the small end of the antler and put it securely in the chuck.

10 Cut a second tenon. Face off the large end of the antler until it is smooth and flat. Turn a tenon about ¼" (6mm) long. This will be threaded during the next step. To determine the diameter of the tenon, measure the inside diameter of the roof opening and add 1/64" (0.4mm). Because the interior of the antler is softer the deeper you go, it often needs to be hardened before it will allow clean, sharp threads to be cut. Flood the tenon with thin cyanoacrylate glue to harden the area to be threaded. Take a light, scraping cut to remove any surplus glue.

11 Cut the threads. Reduce the lathe speed to about 350 rpm and cut the threads in several light passes.

12 **Check the fit of the threads.** Check the fit of the roof on the antler body. At this stage, you want the pieces to fit together so the roof piece barely catches the outside threads of the body tenon. Using the outside threads as a guide, deepen the threads of the body tenon until the roof will thread on.

13 **Harden the threads.** If you removed a good deal of antler during the last step, put some more thin cyanoacrylate glue on the threaded area and let it harden. Clean out the area where the threads come against the shoulder of the antler to give a tight fit.

14 **Adjust the fit.** When the roof threads onto the horn body easily but is not loose, you have a good fit. You will probably need to make many light passes to achieve this fit, often ten or more. Don't rush through the adjustment process, but make the necessary cuts and check the fit often. The fit needs to be just right, not too tight or too loose. Once the threads fit properly, cut a small relief groove so the roof will fit tight against the shoulder of the body. If necessary, make light cuts with a skew chisel in scraping position against the shoulder. This will allow you to adjust the roof's position on the horn body.

15 **Mark and drill the entrance hole.** Mark the entrance hole with a center punch and drill a ¼" (6mm)-diameter hole.

16 **Drill and thread the perch hole.** Drill the perch hole with a #7 drill bit. Then, use a ¼" (6mm)-20 tap drill bit to thread the hole. The hole is tapped because of the off-center location of the hole in the antler body.

17 **Hollow out the body.** Use a negative rake modified scraper to hollow out the body. Use the entrance hole wall thickness as an indicator of the body's wall thickness.

18 **Sand the body.** Sand the shoulder of the body, progressing through various grits of sandpaper up to 400-grit sandpaper.

19 **Polish the top of the body.** Put a drop of friction polish on a rag or paper towel, and wipe the cut surface. Leave the rest of the piece as it is. Turn the lathe on and buff the cut surface, using only one drop of polish at a time.

20 **Wax the roof threads.** Place the chuck holding the roof back on the lathe, and apply a light coat of wax to the threads.

21 **Attach the body.** Thread the antler body onto the roof. The roof will now act as a chuck as you shape the bottom of the body.

22 **Shape and drill the bottom.** Shape the bottom of the body with a ⅜" (10mm) spindle gouge, using the plan for reference. Then, drill a ¼" (6mm) hole in the bottom. Apply thin cyanoacrylate glue to the interior edge of the hole and spray with accelerator. The finial threads will be cut to 5⁄16" (8mm) in diameter using a 20 TPI (teeth per inch) thread chaser.

23 **Thread the finial hole.** Thread the finial hole with smooth, clean threads using a 20 TPI thread chaser. Leave the roof and body in the chuck and set aside.

TURN THE FINIAL

24 **Select the wood and turn and thread a tenon.** Place a ¾" x ¾" x 4" (19 x 19 x 102mm) ebony block in a chuck with extended jaws, leaving about 2" (51mm) of the wood extending out from the jaws. Turn a tenon on the end of the block, and thread it using a 20 TPI thread chaser. Check the tenon frequently for fit against the threaded hole in the bottom of the body. The body will later act as a chuck for turning the finial.

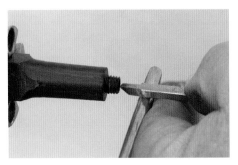

25 **Make a recess.** Create a recess in the end of the finial to house a ⅛" (3mm) turquoise cabochon. This adds interest to the finished ornament.

26 **Glue the cabochon.** Use cyanoacrylate glue to glue the cabochon in place on the end of the finial.

27 **Round the finial.** Reverse the finial in the chuck and turn it to round.

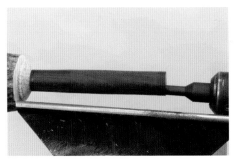

28 **Place the finial.** Remove the round finial from the chuck, and put the chuck with the roof and the body back on the lathe. Screw the finial into the hole in the bottom of the body. Move the revolving center into position to support the end of the finial. The support point may be off center, but turning will bring the long finial into round and it will run true.

29 **Shape the finial.** Start to turn the shape. Work from the small end of the finial and turn toward the headstock, moving from thin wood to heavy wood.

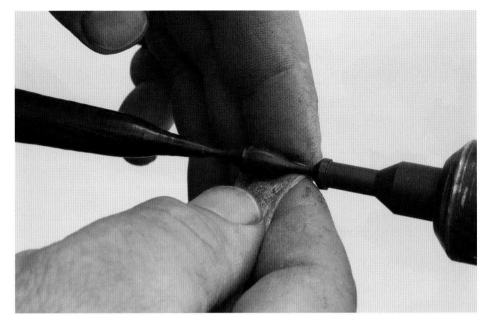

30 **Sand and finish the finial.** Sand the finial, progressing through various grits of sandpaper to 600-grit paper or finer. Finish with light coats of friction polish, buff dry, and apply a light coat of Renaissance wax.

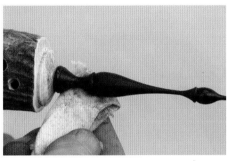

31 **Polish the finial.** Use a soft paper towel to give the finial a final polish.

32 **Part off the finial.** Using the long point of a skew chisel, part off the finial at the small end.

33 **Sand and polish the tip of the finial.** Sand the tip of the finial lightly with 600-grit sandpaper, and then apply a light coat of friction polish.

TURN THE PERCH AND FINISH THE TOP

34 **Select and round the wood.** Place a round piece of ebony in the extended-jaw chuck, and turn it to a cylinder about 1" (25mm) diameter and 1½" to 2" (38 to 51mm) long.

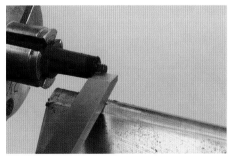

35 **Turn and thread a tenon.** Turn a ⅜" (10mm) tenon and thread it to ¼" (6mm) in diameter with a 20 TPI thread chaser.

36 **Separate the perch.** Using the long point of a skew chisel, make a clean cut to separate the top 1½" (38mm) or so of wood from the end of the block. This piece is the perch that will be threaded into the tapped hole in the body of the ornament. Remove the remaining wood from the chuck.

37 **Turn a mandrel.** Put a cylindrical block 1" (25mm) or larger into the chuck to make a threaded mandrel. Cut threads that will permit the roof to be threaded onto the mandrel to hold it in place as the top is turned.

38 **Shape the top of the roof.** Turn the top of the roof to final shape, leaving enough material for a bead.

39 **Turn the bead.** Turn a bead on the top of the roof. Sand, finish, and drill a hole in the bead large enough to accept a screw eye of your choice.

40 **Sand and finish the roof.** The square edges on the roof need to be sanded flat and smooth. Use a flat block wrapped in sandpaper, progressing through various grits of sandpaper up to 400-grit paper. Apply friction polish and then buff the roof. Place the screw eye in the hole drilled in the roof bead.

41 **Turn the perch.** Thread a 20 TPI hole in the end of the stock left in the chuck (the mandrel from the previous step). Secure the perch in the threaded hole, and turn it to shape with a gouge. Sand the finished piece, progressing through various grits of sandpaper up to 400-grit paper.

42 **Finish the perch.** Apply friction polish to the perch, buff dry, and apply a light coat of wax. Unscrew the perch from the mandrel and screw it into the body of the ornament.

Bark Ornament

I use cottonwood bark for this project, as it turns and carves easily, burns nicely, and has a wonderful, warm finished color.

Designed and carved by Susan L. Hendrix.

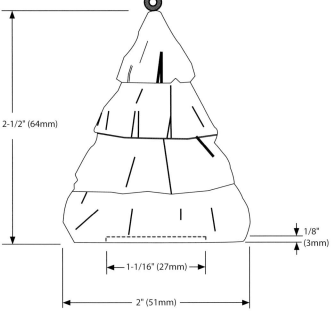

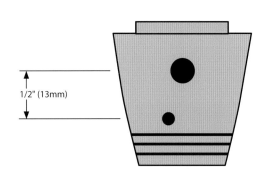

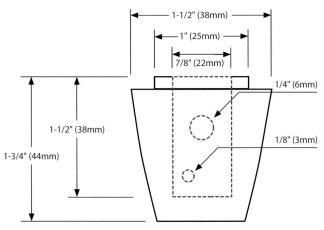

Tools and Materials

- One 2¼" x 2¼" x 2½" (57 x 57 x 64mm) piece of cottonwood bark (roof)
- One 2" x 2" x 2" (51 x 51 x 51mm) piece of ambrosia maple (body)
- Drill bits: ⅛" (3mm), ¼" (6mm)
- Multi-spur bits: ⅞" (22mm), 1⅛" (29mm)
- ⅜" (10mm) spindle gouge
- ½" (13mm) bowl gouge
- Band saw

- Four-jaw chuck
- Drill chuck
- Parting tools
- Skew
- Revolving cone center
- Sandpaper: grits 100, 150, 220, 320
- Carving knife
- Large V-tool
- Mandrel

- Screw eye
- Spray lacquer of choice
- Thin cyanoacrylate glue
- Wire burners
- Safety glove
- Thumb guard
- Woodburner pen with angled tip

The author used these products for the project.
Substitute your choice of brands, tools, and materials as desired.

TURN THE ROOF

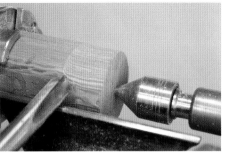

1 Select and mark the bark. Select a sound piece of cottonwood bark large enough to turn a cone shape about 2¼" (57mm) in diameter at the base and 2½" (64mm) tall. Mark a 2⅜" (60mm) circle on the best end of the bark. Use a band saw to remove the excess bark if desired.

2 Round the block. Place the roughly rounded block in a chuck or between centers on the lathe, and turn until it is a cylinder about 2¼" to 2⅜" (57 to 60mm) in diameter.

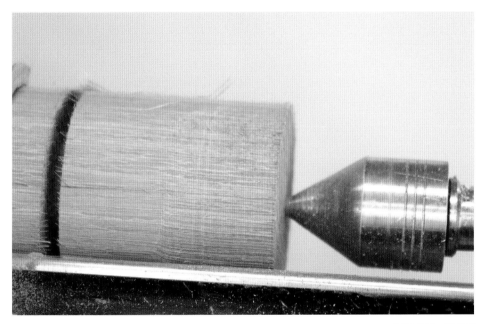

3 Mark the roof height. Face off the end of the cylinder. Then, using a parting tool, cut a line about ¾" (19mm) deep 2½" (64mm) or so from the end of the block. This line will indicate the height of the roof.

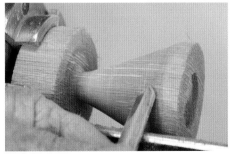

4 Drill a hole for the body. Drill a 1⅛" (29mm) recess about ⅛" (3mm) deep in the end of the cylinder. This recess will be used to center the body on the roof.

5 Shape the roof. Use a ⅜" (10mm) or ½" (13mm) spindle gouge to turn the cylinder to a cone shape, using the line cut during Step 3 as a guide. The finished cone should have a shallow concave curve to the surface.

6 Part off the cone. Using a narrow parting tool, separate the bark cone from the waste stock.

TURN THE BODY

7 **Select and round the wood.** Select a 2" x 2" x 2" (51 x 51 x 51mm) block of figured wood or a piece of wood large enough to create a finished piece 1½" (38mm) in diameter and about 1⅝" (41mm) tall. Secure the block in a chuck, and round the exposed area down to 1½" (38mm) in diameter.

8 **Round the other end and mark the wood.** Reverse the block in the chuck and round the other end, creating a cylinder. Face off the end until the cylinder is about 1⅝" (41mm) long. Mark lines indicating the positions of the entrance and perch holes. These lines should go all the way around the cylinder so you can select the most interesting part of the block and drill the holes there.

9 **Drill the entrance and perch holes.** Drill a ¼" (6mm) hole for the entrance and a ⅛" (3mm) hole for the perch.

10 **Score the top.** Use a 1⅛" (29mm) bit to score a shallow mark on the top of the cylinder. This mark indicates the diameter of the shallow tenon you will turn to align the body and the roof.

11 **Hollow out the body.** Drill a ⅞" (22mm) hole 1¼" (32mm) into the cylinder to hollow it.

12 **Cut the tenon.** Use a parting tool and cut in to the 1⅛" (29mm) line scored on the top of the cylinder to form a tenon. Check the fit against the hole drilled into the roof. Make any adjustments necessary to get a good fit.

13 **Shape the body.** Place the cylinder on a ⅞" (22mm) mandrel, sliding it on as far as it will go. Use a spindle gouge to taper the outside of the cylinder down to about 1⅛" (29mm) at the base.

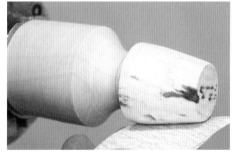

14 **Sand the body.** Sand the body, progressing though various grits of sandpaper and finishing with 320-grit paper.

15 **Score decorative lines.** To add a little interest, use the long point of a skew chisel to score three lines around the bottom of the body about ⅛" (3mm) apart. The scored lines make it easier to friction burn the wood.

16 **Burn the lines.** Use a wire burner to friction burn the lines scored in the bottom of the body. Wire burners are available in various diameters ranging from 0.016" to 0.05" (0.4 to 1mm). The wire pictured is Nichrome (nickel/chromium) wire.

17 **Sand around the lines.** After the lines have been burned in, lightly sand them to help clean and sharpen their appearance.

18 **Finish the body.** Spray the body with two wet coats of finish. If necessary, sand lightly between dry coats.

19 **Shape the roof.** Using a carving knife, shape the roof into a cone shape with a slight inward slope. Carve the tip to a sharp point and then flatten it a bit so a screw eye can be added later. The knife adds texture to the wood and planes to the roof.

20 **Mark the shingles.** Mark shingles on the roof with a pencil. Draw them however you would like, but keep in mind that the smaller the shingles are, the longer it will take you to carve them. The bark has a tendency to break and chip fairly easily, which adds to the rustic look of the finished ornament, so don't worry if this happens as you're carving. If too large a piece breaks off, use some thin cyanoacrylate glue and glue it back in place. Susan likes to carve shingles in a variety of sizes and shapes.

21 **Outline the shingles.** Using a large V-tool, cut along each pencil line to outline the shingles. This separates each individual shingle from the others and starts creating the layered look you want for the finished roof. Lay the V-tool on its side and use the side like a knife, removing the ridges produced when you first outlined the shingles. Separate each layer further by varying the cuts, making some deeper and some more angled.

22 **Finish carving the shingles.** Use a knife to cut the edge of each shingle deeper into the bark. Cut each layer so the bark slopes inward, creating a whimsical look. Continue by undercutting the layers and further separating each individual shingle with knife cuts. Some of the edges will break or chip. If they don't, you can break a few intentionally to make the roof look weathered.

23 **Woodburn the roof.** An angled woodburner pen, shaped like a knife tip, will help you enhance and define each shingle even further. Experiment with the temperature until you get the results you want as each woodburner works a little differently, some burning hotter than others. Susan burns lines randomly under and between the shingles and adds extra lines to the tops and bottoms of the shingle to make them appear to be split. These lines give the roof shadow and depth. Resist the urge to make the lines uniform. Using a variety of temperatures and lines makes the roof look authentic.

24 **Finish the roof.** Spray the roof with a sanding sealer of your choice.

Segmented Ornament

Christmas is a worldwide celebration and this ornament, along with many of the ornaments I create, is made up of segments of rare and exotic woods from all around the world. Incorporating these unique materials in a Christmas ornament represents a celebration of Christmas worldwide. By using different woods, there are countless ways to vary and adapt the design of this project.

Designed and turned by Don Russell. See more of Don's work in the gallery section on page 122.

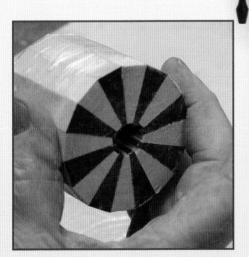

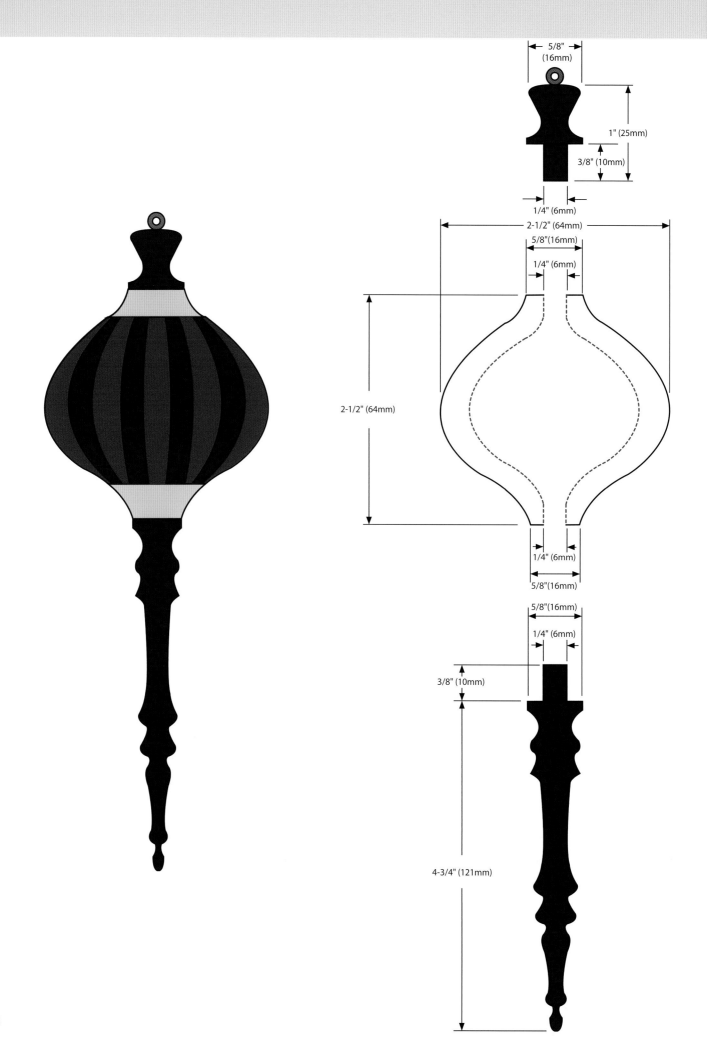

5/8"
(16mm)

1" (25mm)

3/8" (10mm)

1/4" (6mm)

2-1/2" (64mm)

5/8"(16mm)

1/4" (6mm)

2-1/2" (64mm)

1/4" (6mm)

5/8"(16mm)

5/8"(16mm)

1/4" (6mm)

3/8" (10mm)

4-3/4" (121mm)

CUT THE WEDGES

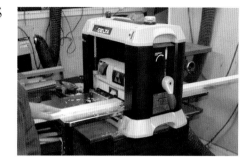

Tools and Materials

- Scrap wood
- Contrasting wood pieces to make the body
- 2 small blocks of wood for the end caps
- One ¾" x ¾" x 8" (19 x 19 x 203mm) piece of wood for the finial and cap
- Thickness planer
- Radial arm saw, table saw, or miter saw
- Rubber mallet
- Plastic square
- Tapered punch
- Side cutting scraper
- Skew
- ¼" (6mm) stove bolt
- Two ¼" (6mm) rubber washers
- ¼" (6mm) wing nut
- ¼" (6mm) open-end wrench
- ¼" (6mm) drill bit
- ¹⁄₁₆" (0.4mm) or smaller drill bit
- ⅜" (10mm) spindle gouge
- Four-jaw chuck
- Long-jaw chuck
- Pen mandrel
- Pen end mill
- ¼" (6mm) extra-long drill bit or ¼" (6mm) brass rod
- ½" (13mm) multi-spur bit
- Drill chuck
- Narrow parting tool
- Sandpaper: grits 80, 100, 150, 220, 320, 400
- Fishhook or screw eye
- 1½" (38mm)-wide masking tape
- Safety stick (shop-made)
- Wood glue
- Packing tape
- Synthetic steel wool
- Spray lacquer of choice
- Sunscreen

The author used these products for the project.
Substitute your choice of brands, tools, and materials as desired.

1 **Prepare the scrap wood.** To start, cut a set-up board from scrap material. Cut several additional scrap boards to the same width and thickness. Run the boards through a planer to ensure the thickness of each one is identical.

2 **Set the saw angle.** You can use a radial arm saw, table saw, or miter saw to cut the wedges for this project. This sequence uses a radial arm saw. The number of wedges you want your ornament to include determines the angle at which you set the saw blade. The ornament in this sequence will have sixteen wedges that form a circle, so the angle of the blade will be set at 11.25º (360º divided by 32, as each wedge has 2 angles). With the saw set at the correct angle, make a cut through the fence and the set-up board. This board should be clamped to the fence to act as the stop block.

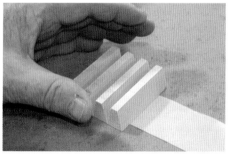

3 **Cut four test wedges.** Make a trial cut into one of the planed scrap boards, and then, flipping the board over each time, cut four wedges. Use a safety stick like the one shown to help hold the wedges during cutting. Lay a strip of masking tape 1½" (38mm) wide sticky side up on your work surface. Place the four wedges side by side on the tape and press them so they stick.

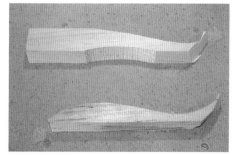

4 **Check the wedges.** Using the masking tape, fold the wedges into a quarter circle. Check this against a square for fit. If necessary, adjust the angle of the saw blade slightly by giving it a light tap with a rubber mallet. Cut four more wedges, and check the measurement again. This process is critical, as the fit of the wedges must be perfect. Continue to move the saw blade slightly to the left or right to get a perfect fit. Make adjustments until the angle of the quarter circle formed by the four wedges is equal to 90º.

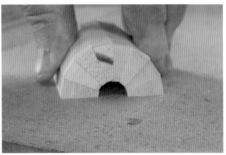

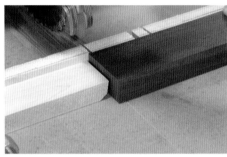

5 **Cut and check eight test wedges.** Cut eight wedges from one of the scrap boards, place them on masking tape, and form a half circle. Check the measurement of the half circle against any flat surface.

6 **Form a circle.** Keep making adjustments and cutting scrap wedges until you have a circle of sixteen wedges that fit together perfectly.

7 **Prepare the project wood.** This segmented ornament will be made from padauk and yellow heartwood. Prepare the material by jointing, planing, and ripping the stock until all the pieces are exactly the same thickness and width and are of an adequate length for the size ornament you want to create.

8 **Cut the project wedges.** Cut eight padauk wedges and eight yellow heart wedges with the saw set to the same angle you used to cut the test wedges.

9 **Make a guide for the wedges.** Place a plastic square on a scrap board. Tape the long side of the square to the board, positioning the tape so that half of it is on the square and half of it is on the board, forming a temporary hinge. Using the tape hinge as a guide, flip the square over. Apply wide masking tape, sticky side down, along the long edge of the square. The majority of the tape should extend past the edge of the square. Using the tape hinge, flip the square back over so the sticky side of the wide masking tape is face up.

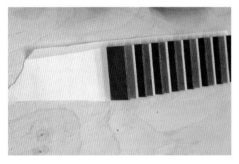

10 **Tape the wedges.** Place the wedges on the piece of wide masking tape, alternating the colors. Use the square to ensure the pieces are placed perfectly straight. Once you have placed all the wedges, peel the tape off the square and trim the excess, leaving only a few inches of tape extending from one end of the line of wedges.

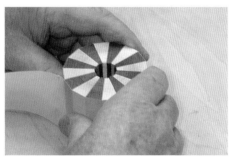

11 **Form a circle.** Roll the wedges into a circle and double-check the fit.

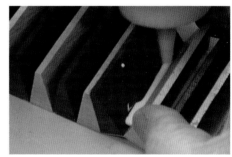

12 **Glue the wedges.** Open the roll and lay the assembly on a flat surface. Place a bead of Titebond glue between each wedge. Be sure to apply glue to the outer edge of one of the end wedges to close up the circle.

13 **Make the final circle.** Roll up the assembly and wrap it tightly with stretchable packing tape. This tape is strong and flexible. Pull it tight so that any excess glue will ooze out of the joints between the wedges.

14 **Check the final assembly.** Drive a tapered punch into the center of the assembly from each side to ensure it is truly round. Set it aside to dry for two or three hours or overnight.

15 **Round the body assembly.** After the glue in the body assembly has set, remove the tape and place the assembly in a four-jaw chuck. Flatten the end of the piece and round it halfway down the side.

16 **Hollow out the body assembly.** Use a side-cutting scraper to hollow out the inside of the assembly. Do not increase the size of the hole at the end of the assembly, but cut away wood from the center. Leave the walls at least ¼" (6mm) thick. Reverse the assembly and repeat the rounding, flattening, and hollowing process. When finished, the assembly should have flat ends and the outside of the piece should be round and smooth.

17 **Bevel the entrance holes.** Using a skew as a scraper, create a bevel around the entry hole on each end of the assembly.

18 **Select and mount an end cap.** Select a piece of wood to be used for the end cap, and mount it in a chuck. Place a spacer behind it so the chuck grips only about ⅛" (3mm) of the end cap piece.

19 **Bevel the end cap.** Use the gouge to cut a bevel on the end of the wood that matches the bevel of one of the body's entrance holes. Smooth the bevel with the skew used as a scraper.

20 **Check and adjust the fit.** Touch one end of the assembly to the spinning end cap with enough force to create a light burn mark. Use a skew to adjust the angle on the end cap until the bevel is the same width as the burn mark. When the bevel and the burn mark are the same widths, the end cap will fit perfectly into the end of the assembly.

21 **Drill the end cap.** Mount a drill chuck in the tailstock, and drill a ¼" (6mm) hole through the end cap. Repeat steps 18–21 to make the second end cap. Cut it to fit the entrance hole on the other end of the body assembly. Mark the end caps and the assembly so you know which cap fits which end of the assembly.

22 **Glue the end caps in place.** Apply glue to the bevels at each end of the assembly. Put the end caps in place, and use a ¼" (6mm) stove bolt, two flat washers, and a wing nut to clamp them in place. Do not clamp the pieces too tightly, but make sure the fit is snug. Set aside for two to three hours or overnight to dry.

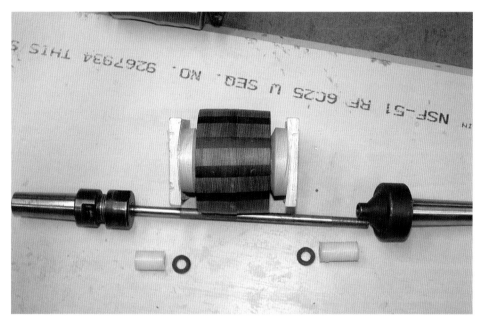

23 **Select a pen mandrel.** To hold the assembly and end caps during turning, you will need a pen mandrel like the one shown. Mount the mandrel on a long ¼" (6mm) drill bit (or ¼" [6mm] brass rod) that will reach through both end caps. The photo sequence will continue using a different assembly than the one pictured during the previous steps, as the original assembly had to be set aside to dry.

24 **Drill holes for the washer and spacer.** Counterbore a flat-bottomed hole in each end cap to receive the mandrel's rubber washer and spacer, which will hold the assembly during final turning. Then select a ¼" (6mm) drill bit or ¼" (6mm) brass rod long enough to reach through both ends, or use an end mill to create a ¼" (6mm) rod long enough to reach through both ends.

25 **Secure the body assembly.** With a spacer and rubber washer in place at each end cap, put the body assembly on the mandrel and secure it between centers.

  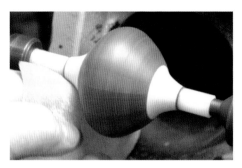

26 **Shape the end caps.** Using a ⅜" (10mm) spindle gouge, remove the excess material from the end caps. Stop when you can see the glue line where the end cap meets the center assembly. Reverse the mandrel and repeat this shaping with the other end cap.

27 **Shape the body.** Turn the assembly and end caps to the final shape, using the plan for reference. Smooth the surface with a skew in scraping position. Continue to turn the end caps down until the rubber washer shows as a black line, indicating the final diameter of the end caps. Continue taking light shaping cuts until the final shape is reached and the surface is acceptable for sanding.

28 **Sand the body.** Sand the body, starting with 80-grit sandpaper and progressing through grits 100, 150, 220, 320, and 400.

29 **Finish the body.** Reduce the lathe speed and spray the body with four coats of fast-drying, lacquer-based sanding sealer. Let dry. Smooth the body with a synthetic steel wool pad such as a Scotch-Brite pad. Then, apply several coats of satin or gloss lacquer, let dry, and smooth again with a synthetic steel wool pad.

30 **Apply sunscreen.** When the finish has dried, coat the body with sunscreen. This provides UV protection and some extra shine.

TURN THE FINIAL AND CAP

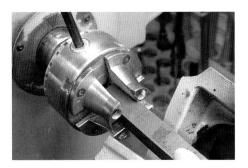

31 **Select and mount the wood.** Mount a ¾" (19mm) square piece of the wood about 8" (203mm) long for the finial. If you use an extended-jaw chuck as shown, there is no need for tailstock support.

32 **Shape the tip.** Start at the end furthest from the chuck and turn the tip detail of the finial, using the plan for reference or turning your own design. When turning a piece like this, always work starting from the end that will have the smaller diameter toward the end that will have the larger diameter.

33 **Finish shaping the finial.** Make clean shearing cuts as the shape forms. Try to turn a pleasing shape with a combination of coves, beads, and tapers. Use the plan for reference. The finial should be larger at the top and gradually taper to a point at the bottom. Round and work one section at a time. The design possibilities are endless.

34 **Cut a tenon.** Cut a ⅜" (10mm)-long tenon at the top of the finial to fit the hole drilled in the end cap at the bottom of the body. Turn the tenon so the diameter is slightly oversized. You will turn it to its final dimensions later.

35 **Sand the finial.** The completed finial should be 5" (127mm) long. Once you are done turning, sand and finish the finial.

36 **Cut the finial tenon to size.** Use a parting tool to turn the finial's tenon to ¼" (6mm) in diameter.

37 **Check the measurement.** Check the diameter of the tenon with a ¼" (6mm) open-end wrench.

38 **Separate the finial.** Using a parting tool, cut the finial from the waste stock.

39 **Face off and drill the remaining stock.** Loosen the chuck and pull the remaining stock out so about 1" (25mm) is exposed. This will be used to turn the ornament cap. Face off the end until it is smooth and flat. Drill a hole in the end of the wood to accommodate a screw eye or other type hanger.

40 **Turn, sand, and finish the cap.** Turn the top cap to a pleasing shape, and turn an oversized tenon on the end. Sand and finish the cap, and then part it off from the waste stock.

41 **Check the fit.** Check the fit of the cap and finial in the end caps of the body. Use a pen end mill to make any adjustments to the ornament body until all the pieces fit properly.

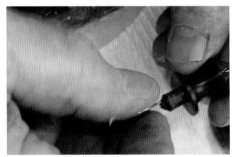

42 **Place the hanger.** Secure the hanger of your choice in the cap. If using a fishhook hanger, bend the fishhook until it is straight and insert it through the cap as shown. Bend the extra length over the tenon, and leave the fishhook eye sticking out the top. Cut off the extra length with a pair of wire cutters.

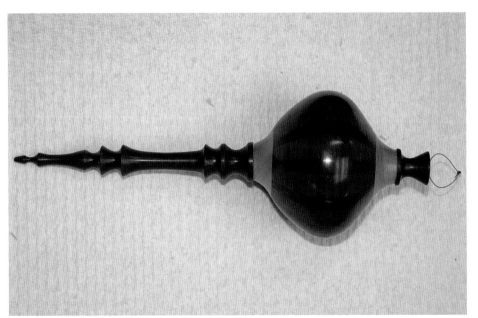

43 **Glue the finial and cap in place.** Glue the finial and cap to the ornament body. Use fishing line to make a loop for hanging the ornament. Red fishing line looks nice on a Christmas ornament.

Sea Urchin Ornament

Sea urchins are round, spine-covered marine animals belonging to the phylum Echinodermata, along with other animals like starfish, sand dollars, and sea cucumbers. Including their spines, sea urchins are typically 2" to 4" in diameter (51 to 102mm). Their spines are often filled with poison and used for protection. Sea urchins also use their spines, and tube feet, to move themselves slowly across the ocean floor. Sea urchins can be found in shades of black, green, brown, purple, white, and red.

During the past few years, some woodturners have combined sea urchin shells with wooden finials to produce very attractive ornaments. I discovered sea urchin shells, sold by the bag, at a craft superstore. I was drawn to their unique shape and developed a pattern to use them in a Christmas ornament design. I gave the sea urchin ornaments I made to my grandchildren.

Designed and turned by Joe Wagner. See more of Joe's work in the gallery section on page 124.

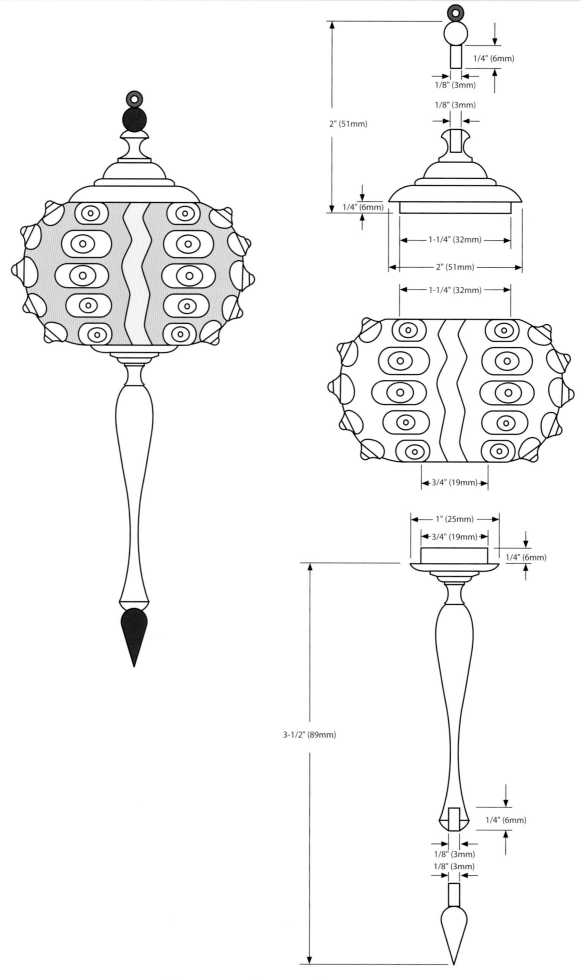

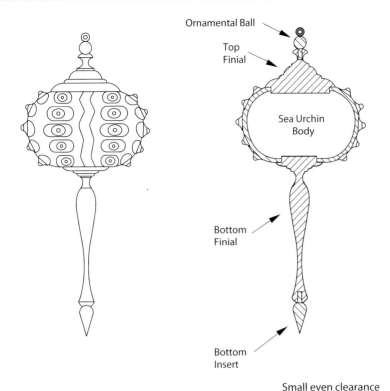

Ornamental Ball

Top Finial

Sea Urchin Body

Bottom Finial

Bottom Insert

Tools and Materials

- Sea urchin shell
- One 2" x 2" x 4" (51 x 51 x 102mm) piece of holly (inserts)
- One 1" x 1" x 8" (25 x 25 x 203mm) piece of holly (finials)
- One ½" x ½" x 4" (13 x 13 x 102mm) piece of holly (ornamental ball)
- One 2½" x 2¼" x 4" (64 x 57 x 102mm) piece of hardwood (step plug gauge)
- Drill bits: ⅛" (3mm), ½" (13mm)
- ¼" (6mm) spindle gouge
- Jacobs or collet chuck
- Calipers
- Parting tools
- Skews
- Revolving cone center
- Steb drive center
- Four-jaw chuck
- Extended-jaw chuck
- Rotary tool (such as those produced by Dremel)
- ½" (13mm) sanding drum
- Ruler
- Sandpaper
- Screw eye
- Wood glue
- Semi-gloss brush lacquer
- Soft cloth
- Paste wax
- 1½" (38mm) nylon rod
- Brush pen
- Synthetic steel wool
- Clear glaze

The author used these products for the project.
Substitute your choice of brands, tools, and materials as desired.

Step	Diameter	Diameter
1	1/2"	13mm
2	5/8"	16mm
3	3/4"	19mm
4	7/8"	22mm
5	1"	25mm
6	1-1/8"	29mm
7	1-1/4"	32mm
8	1-3/8"	35mm
9	1-1/2"	38mm
10	1-5/8"	41mm
11	1-3/4"	44mm
12	1-7/8"	48mm

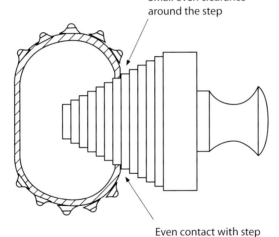

Small even clearance around the step

Even contact with step shoulder on outside surface

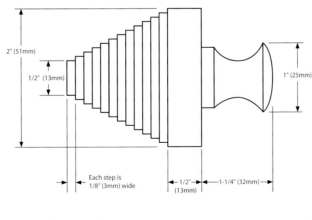

2" (51mm)

1/2" (13mm)

1" (25mm)

Each step is 1/8" (3mm) wide

1/2" (13mm)

1-1/4" (32mm)

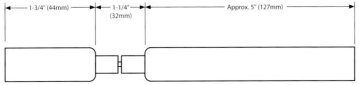

1-3/4" (44mm)

1-1/4" (32mm)

Approx. 5" (127mm)

PREPARE THE SHELL

Since a sea urchin shell is a natural object, the top and bottom openings are irregular in shape. To successfully incorporate a shell in an ornament design, the inside edge of the shell openings need to be prepared to accept a round tenon. In addition, the exterior surface around the openings must be smoothed so the inserts will sit flush on the surface.

1 Turn a step plug gauge. This tool is used to ensure that a good fit is made between the sea urchin and the turned inserts. To make the gauge, mount a 2¼" x 2¼" x 4" (57 x 57 x 102mm) block of hardwood between centers and turn it down to a 2" (51mm) cylinder. Using a sharp ⅛" (3mm)-wide parting tool and a pair of calipers, turn the steps shown in the plan, cutting each step cleanly. After the steps are completed, turn a handle on the end of the gauge. Sand as needed and apply a finish such as Deft lacquer.

2 Round the shell openings. Select a sea urchin shell of the size you prefer. Using a power rotary tool with a ½" (13mm)-diameter sanding drum (such as a Dremel rotary tool), carefully round one of the openings in the shell until one of the steps of the step plug gauge fits into it with a small even clearance. Repeat with the other opening.

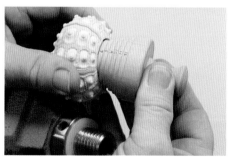

3 Adjust the openings. Insert the step plug gauge into one of the openings, checking for gaps around the edge. Make any adjustments necessary. Be careful when using the step plug gauge, as excessive pressure may damage the shell. If the gauge doesn't fit as well as you would like, continue refining the opening with the rotary tool until you get the proper fit. Repeat with the other opening.

4 Reinforce the shell. Sea urchin shells are quite fragile, so it is a good idea to spray them with a coat or two of heavy bodied lacquer. Use a holder of your choice to hold the shell as you apply the lacquer and allow it to dry.

TURN THE INSERTS

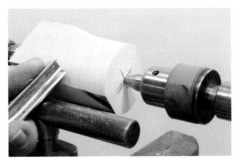

5 **Select and round the wood.** Mount a 2" x 2" x 4" (51 x 51 x 102mm) block of holly between centers. You may use any drive center and revolving center you wish. The setup pictured shows a steb drive center and a cone-point revolving center. Turn the insert blank until it is round and smooth.

6 **Cut a dovetail.** Cut a dovetail on one end of the block, making sure the shoulder of the dovetail is clean and to dimension.

7 **Secure the insert block in a chuck.** Install the dovetail end of the insert block in a chuck, using the tailstock to center it. Tighten the jaws securely.

8 **Measure the shell openings.** Use the step plug gauge to determine the size of the two openings in the shell. The largest opening will be the top of the ornament. You will make an insert to fit the top opening first, and then a second insert to fit the bottom opening.

9 **Transfer the measurement.** Transfer the measurement of the top shell opening from the step plug gauge to a set of calipers. This measurement will be the diameter of the tenon cut in the top insert.

10 **Mark the tenon diameter.** Measure in about ¾" (19mm) from the end of the insert block. Using a parting tool, cut a groove to the set depth of the calipers.

11 **Cut the tenon.** Widen the groove cut during the previous step to make a tenon about ¼" (6mm) long. The ¾" (19mm) length of wood left to one side of the tenon will be turned and shaped to form the top insert.

12 **Shape the top insert.** Turn the exterior shape of the insert, leaving a lip that is approximately ¼" (6mm) larger in diameter than the tenon. Undercut the lip slightly so the glue will not ooze onto the surface of the ornament during assembly.

13 **Mark the top insert.** Using the tip of a small skew, make a center mark in the top of the insert to help center the drill bit.

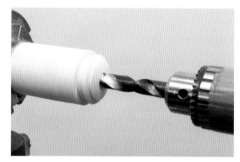

14 **Drill a hole for the top finial.** Mount a ½" (13mm) drill bit in a drill chuck (like a Jacobs chuck) in the lathe tailstock. Drill a hole in the end of the insert, making sure it is deep enough to pass through the entire insert once the insert has been separated from the waste stock.

15 **Sand and finish the insert.** Sand the outside of the insert, progressing through various grits of sandpaper up to 600-grit paper. Apply a coat of semi-gloss lacquer, and buff dry with a clean cloth using moderate pressure.

16 **Smooth the insert.** If you can feel any rough spots on the surface of the wood, buff it with synthetic steel wool to get a glossy smooth surface.

17 **Polish the insert.** Give the insert a light coat of paste wax, and buff it with a soft cloth.

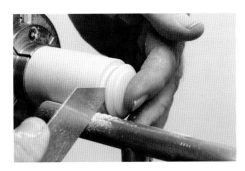  

18 **Separate the insert.** Use a parting tool to cut the insert free, leaving approximately ⅛" to ³⁄₁₆" (3 to 5mm) of the tenon extending past the lip.

19 **Check the fit.** Check the fit of the insert against the top opening in the shell. If necessary, make adjustments to the top opening to get a nice fit.

20 **Glue the insert.** Glue the insert in place, placing a light bead of glue around the inside edge of the top opening. As you put the insert in place, rotate it to distribute the glue evenly around the contact area. Repeat steps 5–20 to turn and place the bottom insert.

21 **Determine the finial length.** With the inserts glued in place, use a ruler to estimate the length of the top and bottom finials. A 1" x 1" x 8" (25 x 25 x 203mm) cylinder should provide enough wood to turn both finials.

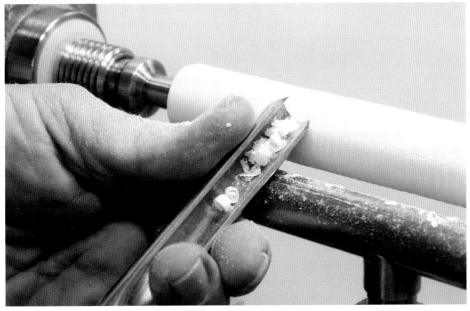

22 **Mount and round the finial block.** Mount a 1" x 1" x 8" (25 x 25 x 203mm) block of wood between centers, and turn it to a cylinder. Face off both ends.

TURN THE FINIALS

23 **Mark the length of the bottom finial.** Determine how long you would like the bottom finial to be. In this example it is about 3½" (89mm) long. Mark the dimension on the cylinder, adding a little extra length to allow for cutting and finishing.

24 **Set a pair of calipers to the proper measurement.** Use a ½" (13mm) drill bit to set a pair of calipers to a width of ½" (13mm).

25 **Cut a tenon for the bottom finial.** Use a parting tool and the calipers to make a cut where you marked the end of the bottom finial on the cylinder, cutting until you reach a diameter of ½" (13mm). Widen this cut to form a tenon about 1¼" (32mm) long.

26 **Cut two partial bead shapes.** Use a small gouge to roll a ½" (13mm) partial bead shape on each side of the tenon, undercutting slightly. You want to complete this step now, as you will have limited access to this area later in the process.

27 **Separate the cylinder.** Using a narrow parting tool, make a cut halfway along the length of the tenon, cutting almost the whole way through the wood.

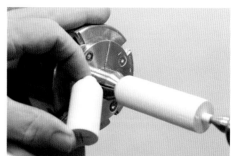

28 **Separate the finial pieces.** Remove the cylinder from the lathe and snap it into two pieces at the parting groove. The smaller piece is the blank for the top finial, and the larger piece is the blank for the bottom finial.

29 **Shape the bottom tip.** Install a ½" (13mm) Jacobs chuck or another suitable chuck (such as the collet chuck pictured). Insert the ½" (13mm)-diameter tenon of the bottom finial blank into the chuck. Bring the tailstock up to the end for support and tighten the chuck. Turn the finial, shaping the tip to final shape.

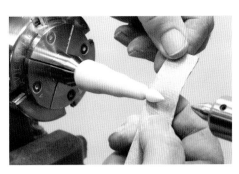

30 **Sand the bottom tip.** Sand the tip of the finial using various grits of sandpaper up through 600-grit paper.

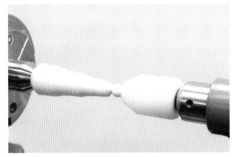

31 **Make a stabilizer.** Before the rest of the finial is turned, it is good practice to make a stabilizer that will accept the bulbous end of the finial and will fit over the end of the revolving center. The one pictured is made from a 1½" (38mm) nylon rod that has been drilled to fit over the revolving center on one end and to fit the diameter of the finial's tip on the other end. The stabilizer's function is to support the end of the finial during the final shaping.

32 **Turn and sand the bottom finial.** Turn the bottom finial to final shape. Sand it using various grits of sandpaper up through 600-grit paper. Leave the stabilizer in place for most of the sanding, but remove it to give the tip a final sanding. Support the tip with your fingers and gently sand it to final smoothness.

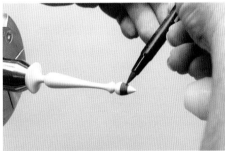

33 **Color the tip.** Color the tip of the bottom finial with a brush pen, such as a Tombow Dual Brush Pen. Use the color of your choice, or leave the tip of the finial unpainted.

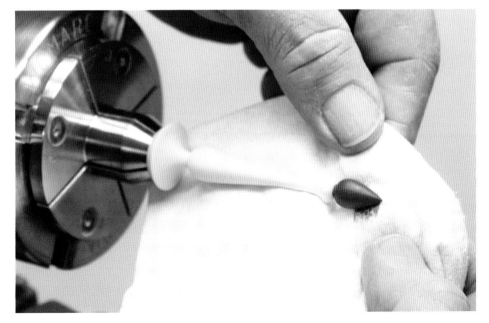

34 **Buff the tip.** Once the paint has been applied, use a soft paper towel to gently buff the finial tip.

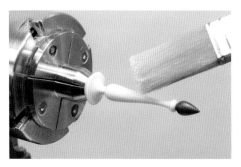

35 **Finish the bottom finial.** Apply a coat of semi-gloss lacquer to the bottom finial, wait a few minutes, and then buff it dry.

36 **Check the fit.** Place the finial in the bottom insert to check the fit. Make any adjustments necessary to achieve a proper fit.

37 **Turn the top finial.** Insert the ½" (13mm)-diameter tenon of the top finial into the chuck. Bring the tailstock up for support and tighten the chuck. Turn the top finial to shape.

38 **Mark the top finial.** Using the tip of a small skew chisel, make a center mark in the top of the finial.

39 **Drill, sand, and finish the top finial.** Drill a ⅛" (3mm)-diameter hole about ½" (13mm) into the top of the finial. Chamfer, or bevel, the edge of the hole using a skew chisel held on its side. Sand the top finial using various grits of sandpaper up through 600-grit. Apply a coat of semi-gloss lacquer and buff dry with a clean cloth using moderate pressure.

40 **Glue the top finial.** Check the fit of the top finial against the top insert and make any necessary adjustments. When satisfied, glue the top finial in place.

41 **Turn an ornamental ball.** Mount a ½" x ½" x 4" (13 x 13 x 102mm) block in a chuck, and turn a ball about ⁷⁄₁₆" (11mm) in diameter with a ⅜" (10mm)-long tenon that is ⅛" (3mm) in diameter.

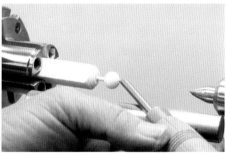

42 **Mark the ornamental ball.** Hold a small skew chisel on its side and make a small dimple on the top of the ball for centering a drill bit.

43 **Drill a hole for the screw eye.** Using the centering mark from the previous step as a guide, drill a hole in the top of the ornamental ball large enough to accommodate a screw eye.

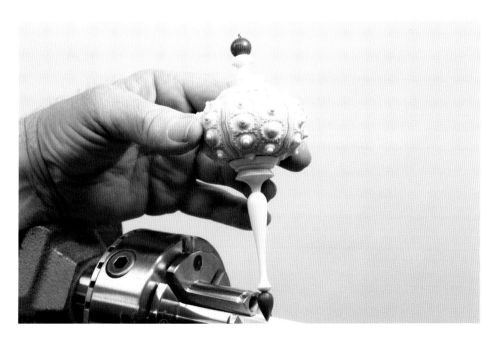

44 **Finish and glue the ornamental ball.** Using the same method you did to color and buff the tip of the bottom finial, color and buff the ornamental ball. When finished, insert the screw eye in the top of the ball. Glue the ball in place at the top of the ornament.

Gallery

Here you will find some beautiful ornaments made by a group of fantastic turners. Let these designs inspire you and spark your imagination as you design and turn your own ornaments.

DAVE BEST

Dave Best has been a hobby woodworker throughout his adult life. He began woodturning in 2004, purchasing his first lathe with the intent of pushing furniture making to a new level. Initially, he had no idea how fulfilling woodturning items other than furniture could be, but he has since explored a range of turning projects. Soon after he began turning, Best joined the Utah Association of Woodturners. He served as the president of the group from July 2006, to June 2010. During that time, he participated in monthly demonstration meetings presented by various group members and acted as a primary teacher during monthly training meetings, teaching turning techniques and processes such as turning beads and coves, bowl coring, chucking, and simple tool making. During his time as president, Best also started producing videos of the monthly demonstrations. These videos are still available for purchase at very reasonable price. In 2011, Best was a demonstrator at the Utah Woodturning Symposium. He has also produced a commercial DVD on the subject of making bat houses. The following are variations on Best's Bat House Ornament, presented on page 67, and were all turned in Spring 2011.

Made of chakte viga and Gaboon ebony, the body of this ornament was turned to resemble a butternut squash, with the short finial at the base of the ornament forming the dried flower found at the base of the squash. The witch's hat roof, perch, and finial were all made of Gaboon ebony.

This piece features highly figured chakte viga (witch's hat roof) and uses thirteen pieces of Gaboon ebony alternated with thirteen pieces of veneer, dyed orange, to form the body. The body shape was turned to resemble a classic fall pumpkin.

Thirteen pieces of chakte viga and thirteen pieces of veneer, dyed black, form the cylindrical body of this ornament.

This ornament is a spin on the one presented on page 67. It utilizes six pieces of Gaboon ebony alternated with six pieces of Chakte viga.

RON BROWN

Ron Brown is an active member of the woodworking community, founding both the Gwinnett Woodworkers Association and the Atlanta Scrollsaw Club, and a member of the American Association of Woodturners. He has experience with trim carpentry, cabinetmaking, furniture making, and woodturning and has been sharing his knowledge with others for more than forty years. He has given demonstrations at turning events across the country and is a featured demonstrator on "The Woodworking Show." In addition to his work as a demonstrator, Brown is the designer of the Longworth Chuck. He has also produced multiple how-to instructional videos on woodturning and scrollsawing, which can be viewed on YouTube. To learn more, visit *www.coolhammers.com*.

Spalted Splendor, 2005. Spalted beech globe with maple top and finial. Don Russell's polychromatic vase class in Georgia inspired the design for this and the other ornaments in Brown's gallery.

Icicles on Display, 2005. Ipê globe with bloodwood top and finial. The decorative elements on the globe are ash over black dyed veneer.

Dot Flower Power, 2005. Ipê globe with bloodwood top and finial. The decorative elements on the globe feature a walnut/maple background with lacewood, and maple and yellowheart flowers.

Dot Flower Under Powered, 2005. Ipê globe with bloodwood top and finial. The globe's decorative elements include a walnut background with lacewood and yellowheart and purpleheart flowers over maple veneer.

KIRK DEHEER

Kirk DeHeer has been sharing his extensive woodturning knowledge with others for years, working as a workshop assistant and now a resident instructor at Craft Supplies USA. DeHeer gives his students a strong understanding of woodturning fundamentals so they can go on to apply their skills to a great variety of woodturning techniques and projects. DeHeer is known as one of the best tool sharpeners in the business and has demonstrated his sharpening and other woodturning techniques at shows and symposiums throughout the United States. All the ornaments shown were turned in 2011, and all the parts are threaded together.

DeHeer used kingwood to turn the top, finial, and perch of this ornament, and elk antler for the body.

Black and white ebony form the top, perch, and finial of this ornament, with the body made of elk antler.

This ornament has a cocobolo top, finial, and perch, with an elk antler body.

The top, finial, and perch of this ornament feature tulipwood, while the body is made of deer antler.

CINDY DROZDA

Through her first job at a piano factory, Cindy Drozda has a basic understanding of woodworking, metal machining, brazing, plastics, adhesives, fasteners, engineering, and machining. Her true passion, though, has always been woodworking, and she made her first woodturned piece in 1984. Drozda, an active member of the American Association of Woodturners, has had her work featured in exhibitions and shows throughout the country and is often asked to demonstrate her techniques. She has appeared in several magazines and books and has a series of instructional DVDs. Drozda lives in Boulder, Colorado, with her life partner, David, and three cats. To learn more, visit *www.cindydrozda.com*.

This ornament features a sea urchin shell gilded with metal leaf. An African blackwood top and finial complete the piece, which is part of Drozda's *Sea Urchin Series*.

Part of Drozda's *Sea Urchin Series*, this ornament is made of a sea urchin shell with a black acacia top and finial.

ALAN LELAND

Alan Leland was born in Florida, grew up in Connecticut, and attended school in North Carolina where he now lives. After graduating from college, Leland began working at a furniture company in Raleigh, making crate-style furniture. This sparked his interest in joinery and crafted furniture, and he began to study books, magazines, and TV shows about woodworking, eventually gathering his own set of tools and experimenting with various joinery techniques. Leland became an active member of several woodworking clubs, including the Triangle Woodturners of North Carolina and the Carolina Mountian Woodturners, where he discovered his passion for woodturning. Leland went on to join the American Association of Woodturners (AAW) and start his own company, Sliding Dovetail Woodworks, which focused on building custom furniture and woodturning. The company is now known as Leland Studios, and maintains a focus on teaching classes and sharing knowledge of woodworking and turning with others. Leland has recently developed a woodturning lab manual, which will be available through the AAW's website. The manual works in conjunction with the weeklong classes Leland teaches as the John C. Campbell Folk School. To learn more, visit *http://alanleland.com.*

Hollow Globe Ornament Rosewood Burgundy Dymondwood, 2011. Big leaf maple burl globe with rosewood burgundy dymonwood top and finial. Leland places great importance on the construction of his ornaments. He carefully measures the diameter of his cap and finial pieces to ensure they are of the proper proportions when compared to the ornament's globe. He also works with the cap and finial pieces to blend them with the curvature of the globe. These details make Leland's pieces incredibly appealing to the eye.

Spalted Pink Ivory Ornament, 2012. Spalted pink ivory globe with ebony cap and finial. As with most of Leland's hollow globe ornaments, the globe of this piece is turned to a squashed shape. The final spherical shape is made by adding the cap and finial pieces, which Leland turns to match and/or enhance the curve of the globe. Leland turned flat edged plates on the cap and finial pieces, finding the flat edge provides a softer visual effect and is also more challenging to turn.

BOB ROSAND

Pennsylvania resident Robert Rosand started working with wood in his youth and has turned his passion into a lifelong career. Author of numerous woodturning articles in *American Woodturner* magazine, Rosand has been teaching, writing, and demonstrating woodturning techniques for more than thirty years. He is a member of the American Association of Woodturners, having formerly served as vice president and a member of the board of directors. Rosand has led demonstrations at local and national woodturning shows and symposiums throughout the United States and has had pieces placed in several exhibitions throughout the country. His works have been purchased for inclusion in private collections in the United States, Europe, and Japan. Additionally, a Christmas ornament turned by Rosand and painted by his wife, Susan, was chosen to be among the decorations placed on one of the White House Christmas trees. Susan is a talented artist and often collaborates with Rosand to produce one-of-a-kind pieces.

Bell Ornament. Turned by Bob Rosand; painted in oils by Susan Rosand.

Country Christmas. Turned by Bob Rosand; painted in oils by Susan Rosand.

Burl Globe. Rosand used an Optivisor magnifier and a .005 Pigma Micron pen to write a passage from the gospel according to Luke in miniature on this ornament.

Here Fishy, Fishy. Rosand used a woodburner with a fish scale tip to add the pattern to the globe of this ornament.

DON RUSSELL

Don Russell has forty years of woodworking knowledge, and experience teaching both children and adults. His skills include building furniture and museum exhibits, repairing antiques, and woodturning. He combined his interest in geometry with his woodturning expertise to create a method for making segmented, staved turnings. Russell enjoys sharing his knowledge with others, having taught classes in Cobb County, Georgia, through the community school program, and more recently at the John C. Campbell Folk School in Brasstown, North Carolina. Russell has been involved with several woodturning organizations, including the Woodworkers Guild of Georgia (president for two years), the Peach State Woodturners (founding member), and the American Association of Woodturners.

These ornaments demonstrate Russell's skill at segmented turning, incorporating several different color arrangements and patterns. These ornaments follow the theme of Russell's step-by-step project (page 91) as an exploration of Christmas as a worldwide celebration.

Joe Wagner

Joe Wagner has more than forty years of woodworking experience and is best known for his unique ability to develop tools to aid in the creation of his woodturning projects. His famous Wagner Texturing Tools are knurling tools that incorporate toothed wheels for adding textures or patterns to wood. Wagner also has a passion for sharing his knowledge with others and teaches woodturning classes that explore various woodturning techniques. Wagner has a particular knack for creating striking ornaments and small-scale projects of unique beauty.

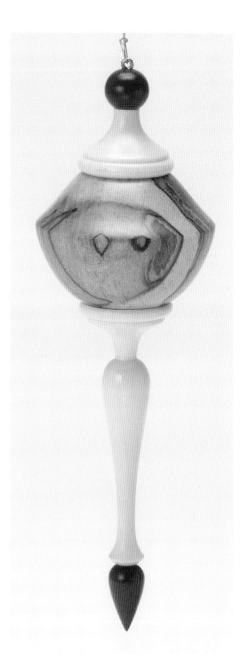

Cherry forms the "nut" of this acorn birdhouse. The ornament is completed with a walnut cap and a top ball and perch of African blackwood. Wagner developed a texturing tool specifically to add the pattern you see on the acorn's cap.

The lighting fixtures in the parking lot of a craft store Wagner's wife likes to frequent inspired the design for this and the following ornament. The globe is hollow ambrosia maple, and the top and bottom finials are made of holly. Wagner used a brush pen to color the tips of the finials.

This ornament features an ambrosia maple globe with kingwood finials.

This snowman is one of Wagner's favorite creations and features a holly body, dyed sugar maple hat, twisted wire arms, and a ribbon scarf.

Index

Note: Page numbers in *italics* indicate step-by-step projects.

A
acorn birdhouse, 124
ambrosia ornaments, *31–38*, 124–25

B
Bark Ornament, *85–90*
Bat House Ornament, *67–75*
Bell Ornament (Rosands), 120
Best, Dave, *67–75*, 113
birdhouse ornaments
  about: reasons for, 9
  2000 Ornament, *19–26*
  2003 Mushroom Ornament, *27–31*
  2004 Ambrosia Ornament, *31–38*
  2005 Natural Edge Ornament, *39–46*
  2006 Feeder Ornament, *47–52*
  2007 Pagoda Ornament, *53–59*
  2010 Ornament, *60–65*
  acorn birdhouse, 124
  cardinal houses, 118
book overview, 8
Brown, Ron, 114–15
Burl Globe (Rosand), 121

C
cardinal houses, 118
Country Christmas (Rosands), 121

D
DeHeer, Kirk, *76–84*, 116–17
Dot Flower Power (Brown), 115
Dot Flower Under Powered (Brown), 115
Drozda, Cindy, 118

E
elk horn ornaments, *76–84*, 116–17

F
feeder ornament, *47–52*
finials, 14–16

G
gallery, 112–25
  Best, Dave, 113
  Brown, Ron, 114–15
  DeHeer, Kirk, 116–17
  Drozda, Cindy, 118
  Holtus, Pete, 118
  Leland, Alan, 119
  Rosand, Bob (with Susan Rosand), 120–21
  Russell, Don, 122–23
  Wagner, Joe, 124–25

H
Halloween ornaments, *67–75*, 113
Hendrix, Susan L., ornament, *85–90*
Here Fishy, Fishy (Rosand), 121
Hollow Globe Ornament Rosewood Burgundy Dymondwood (Leland), 119
Holtus, Pete, 118

I
Icicles on Display (Brown), 114

L
Leland, Alan, 119

M
mandrels, 12–13
mushroom ornament, *27–31*

N
natural edge ornament, *39–46*

O
ornament projects. *See also* birdhouse
ornaments
Bark Ornament, *85–90*
Bat House Ornament, *67–75*
Sea Urchin Ornament, *101–11*
Segmented Ornament, *91–100*
Threaded Elk Horn Ornament, *76–84*

P
pagoda ornament, *53–59*
projects. *See* birdhouse ornaments;
ornament projects; *specific projects
(page numbers in italics)*
pumpkin ornament, 113

R
Rosand, Bob (with Susan Rosand), 120–
21
Russell, Don, *91–100*, 122–23

S
sea urchin ornaments, *101–11*, 118
Segmented Ornament, *91–100*
Spalted Pink Ivory Ornament (Leland),
119
Spalted Splendor (Brown), 114

T
templates, 11
Threaded Elk Horn Ornament, *76–84*
tools, 11
turning tricks
finials, 14–16
finishing, 17
mandrels, 12–13
templates, 11
tools, 11
2000 Ornament, *19–26*
2003 Mushroom Ornament, *27–31*
2004 Ambrosia Ornament, *31–38*
2005 Natural Edge Ornament, *39–46*
2006 Feeder Ornament, *47–52*
2007 Pagoda Ornament, *53–59*
2010 Ornament, *60–65*

W
Wagner, Joe, *101–11*, 124–25
worldwide ornaments, *91–100*, 122–23

Acquisition editor: Peg Couch

Copy editors: Paul Hambke and Heather Stauffer

Cover and page designer: Ashley Millhouse

Layout designer: Wil Younger

Step-by-step photographer: Susan L. Hendrix

Gallery photographer: Jason Anderson

Editor: Katie Weeber

Proofreader: Lynda Jo Runkle

Indexer: Jay Kreider

More Great Books from Fox Chapel Publishing

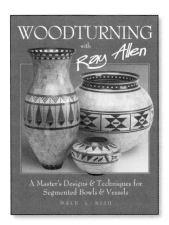

Woodturning with Ray Allen
ISBN 978-1-56523-217-4 $24.95

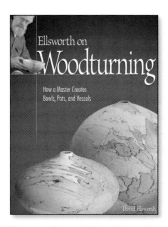

Ellsworth on Woodturning
ISBN 978-1-56523-377-5 $29.95

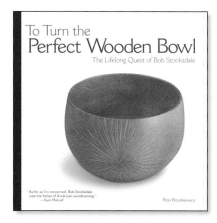

**To Turn the Perfect
Wooden Bowl**
ISBN 978-1-56523-388-1 **$24.95**

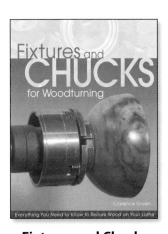

**Fixtures and Chucks
for Woodturning**
ISBN 978-1-56523-519-9 **$22.95**

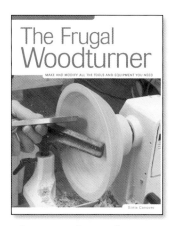

The Frugal Woodturner
ISBN 978-1-56523-434-5 **$19.95**

**Woodturning Today: A
Dramatic Evolution**
ISBN 978-1-56523-587-8 **$27.95**

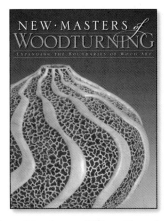

New Masters of Woodturning
ISBN 978-1-56523-334-8 **$29.95**

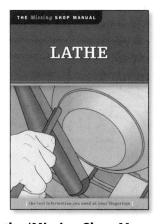

Lathe (Missing Shop Manual)
ISBN 978-1-56523-470-3 **$12.95**

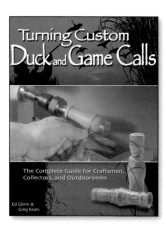

**Turning Custom Duck
and Game Calls**
ISBN 978-1-56523-281-5 **$19.95**